I0450211

END
STATES

Why diverse societies thrive, and why systems of order
lead to collapse

Ben Wallace

Published by BANG Books
San Francisco, CA 94103, USA

First published in the United States of America
by BANG Books, 2015

Copyright Benjamin Edward Wallace, 2015
All rights reserved

If you can't buy me, find me online

"If it weren't for the people, the god-damn people", said Finnerty, "always getting tangled up in the machinery. If it weren't for them, the world would be an engineer's paradise."
— Kurt Vonnegut, 'Player Piano'

In the beginning

In the beginning was the Word.

Actually, in the beginning we don't really know what there was. We don't even know if our beginning was the beginning, or one of many beginnings.

Our best guess is that in the beginning there was some kind of singularity - that at the centre of our universe was a point of infinitely dense, uniform, spinning black sameness, where everything was alike, and contained, and restrained by one almighty unified force. Now, for some reason this singular spinning top got knocked off its axis, and with a Big Bang its infinite density and order exploded forth into the universe. Over time the one thing became everything: energy, protons, neutrons, electrons, hydrogen, helium, super-hot plasma and gas, stars, quasars, galaxies and superclusters. Eventually it became rocks, and planets, and lava and ice and liquid water, and somehow amoeba and plants and trees and insects and fish and warthogs and Kid Rock and Bananagrams and, well, you get the idea.

The fact that we can get the idea is magical. The fact that one massive fiery explosion and billions of years of random collisions and chance galactic encounters later we can sit here and comprehend a universe forming - whilst vast clouds of water vapor sail through a blue sky above us, and small feathered animals sing to each other in the trees - is almost beyond comprehension itself.

The almost infinite complexity of the whole thing, and the apparent randomness that led to a universe so vast, mysterious and beautiful is - for me - the cosmological proof for why Difference, and not uniformity, is the prevailing force for creation and growth in our world and in our lives. If you're a religious person I'm sure you need little convincing of the endless wonder and variety in creation. If you aren't, then the empirical, scientific approach to understanding our origins is just as marvelous.

Adaptation, and being different from what came before, allowed protozoan bacteria - through generations of multiplication and mutation - to become complex; to grow cilia so they could move, fins so they could swim and, eventually, limbs and lungs that let them emerge from the water. Recognising difference in shape and colour is what allows all of us to make sense of our world, and the difference of one moment to the next - of one day being different from any other - is what makes us feel alive. In no uncertain terms, difference is what gives everything in our world and our universe meaning.

Strange, then, that although our universe grows ever more vast, complex and different as it expands through space, we as human beings are creatures of such habit and control. In opposition to the systems we observe - the collapsing stars and eroding coastlines which tend towards chaos and destruction - we devote our energy to building structure. We are comforted by routine; rigorously taxonomising our planets and butterflies. We create layer upon layer of order where there was no order before, and expend vast amounts of effort just holding it all together.

Human beings - who are least distressed when they can see things in black and white or right and wrong - seem like a walking contradiction. Like all animals we thrive and grow from the unexpected and diverse experiences that we have in our lives. We know that discovery and adversity fuel us and yet - at the self-proclaimed top of the food chain - we try our darndest to stamp out the possibility that anything unexpected will happen. I'm not talking about war, or drought, or any of the long list of man-made or natural disasters that come out of the blue and devastate lives and communities. I'm also not talking about the immediate, urgent challenges we might have to deal with in our lives, like finding our lost child in a supermarket, or planning our monthly budget so we can pay rent.

What I wonder at are the long, slow, large-scale changes, which build up sometimes over generations: the constricting systems that shape our lives over decades and centuries. How our education systems, for example, are structured so much like our penal systems, to promote uniformity and to marginalise deviant ways of thinking, or to sideline them with labels like "autistic". And the intransigent, entrenched prejudice to which low politics panders; demonising foreign faces, unknown religions, accents, ethnicities and tastes.

Like lots of people who write about Life, the Universe &

Everything, I wonder a lot. I wonder why we outlaw homosexuality. I wonder how it can be right to ban public protest. I wonder if they'll ever make a true spiritual sequel to the Jean-Claude Van Damme Street Fighter movie. I've wondered at the Rat Race of our grown-up lives; the airless, grey, cubicled daily trudge into which billions of us collectively pour trillions of hours of our collective existence.

As we answer emails, fill in spreadsheets and fiddle with our ties we are all pursuing something, but for each of us that something is different. In a world of infinite diversity, where we're all born different into a world that is never the same one minute to the next - born with different desires and aspirations - can we honestly say that the systems we've set up around ourselves really match the desires we nurtured as younger people? Are they worthy of the vast opportunity for joy and discovery which is out there, outside of the cubicle? Quite the opposite.

If I'd titled this book Fear of a Midlife Crisis instead of End States it would have sounded less pretentious, but the other words in the book wouldn't have had to change that much. If you're like me, then pretty much every time you take a week off from work and go on a long hike, take a walk along a deserted beach or stay up late at night after drinking too much coffee, you get that "What the #$%@! am I doing with my life?" feeling; the feeling that if you could just extricate yourself from your desk job, or your mortgage, or your expectant parents, or the feelings of inadequacy that you get when you see your friends' shiny new husbands and jobs and Facebook statuses, then you might be able to pursue what you'd always wanted to do. Like me, you may also find it harder and harder as the days and pay grades and dentist's appointments go by, to remember what that thing was in the first place.

For almost all of us (myself included) it's impossible and irresponsible to shrug off all the responsibilities and expectations that are built up around us. We can't escape the motions we have to go through, and the processes and systems we have to follow. I'll be honest, in a year's time you'll probably still need to fill in your tax return, and you'll probably still have to queue for 45 minutes to post a Christmas card, or get a new passport. But that doesn't stop us from being able to change things. It doesn't stop us from being able to #occupy public spaces en masse, to anonymously expose corruption, or for individuals within those systems to expose abuses (Snowden, Manning etc.). Although so many of our paths - through airport check-in, at border crossings and at the DMV when we get our drivers' licences - seem inevitable and set in stone, it really only seems that way. Once upon a time they didn't exist at all, and it was a fallible human being, probably just winging it, who was responsible for making them.

I don't subscribe to much New Age Philosophy, but I do know there's a Cosmic Difference inherent in the universe, and millions of people praying for fewer office jobs and grey days in their lives, and they're imploring you to believe things can be different, and be better for being different. Believing has to be the first step - in many ways it is a giant leap.

In pursuit of understanding what 'Difference' means in society, and why it is fundamentally a force for positive change, I'm going to ask you to accept three different principles. One is the necessity of nonconformism; that questioning dogma and institutions is vital, and that the more entrenched something is, the more we should question why it is the way it is. The second is letting your own identity shape your life - recognising what your core, personal values are, and that they are not the barrage of mass media slogans and advertising that you receive every day of your life. The third, and hardest, is to believe that there is no one truth in any situation. Our differing life experiences give us different perspectives, and although we feel passionately a sense of right and wrong, it is empathy - understanding why other people believe what they do - and not preaching, which allows us to come to understanding. Difference, even difference of opinion, can always be celebrated for the new perspective it brings us, even if we passionately disagree.

Entertaining these ideas - even just keeping them at the back of your mind, or on flash cards in your pocket - means we can start to reform some of the unpleasant, entrenched things today that we grudgingly accept about the world we live in, but which we wish we could change. Before we dive in, though, let's try and understand what's going on here. In a world of vast oceans, jungles, dolphins, bungee jumping and chocolate hobnobs, how did all the stuff that makes us feel glad to be alive get relegated to such a small portion of our existence. How did the world we built around ourselves begin to get in the way?

The Pursuit of Happiness

In wealthy Europe and America at least, part of the problem was that a lot of people actually got everything that the primitive animal parts of their brains wanted. We got a roof over our heads, a cheap supply of sugary, salty and fatty foods, and somewhere to hang out 9-5 that kept us out of mischief on the streets. And now, like every empire that's striven and risen and fallen, it feels a bit like we're waddling into irrelevancy; too flabby to keep up with a global economy; an ascendant China and south-east Asia. This is certainly a view that writer John Steinbeck took, writing to a friend in 1959 about (among other things) a pet parrot:

Adlai, do you remember two kinds of Christmases? There is one kind in a house where there is little and a present represents not only love but sacrifice. The one single package is opened with a kind of slow wonder, almost reverence. Once I gave my youngest boy, who loves all living things, a dwarf, peach-faced parrot for Christmas. He removed the paper and then retreated a little shyly and looked at the little bird for a long time. And finally he said in a whisper, "Now who would have ever thought that I would have a peach-faced parrot?"

Then there is the other kind of Christmas with present piled high, the gifts of guilty parents as bribes because they have nothing else to give. The wrappings are ripped off and the presents thrown down and at the end the child says—"Is that all?" Well, it seems to me that America now is like that second kind of Christmas. Having too many

things they spend their hours and money on the couch searching for a soul. A strange species we are. We can stand anything God and nature can throw at us save only plenty. If I wanted to destroy a nation, I would give it too much and would have it on its knees, miserable, greedy and sick.
- John Steinbeck, Guy Fawkes Night, 1959

Steinbeck's son is amazed by his parrot. It is unique and it is new. But Steinbeck's country - the USA - is already sinking into apathy. With every material whim granted, and less and less to struggle for, there's less to aspire to, and less that is special. America, for Steinbeck, is sick with excess.

There a definite truth in Steinbeck's observation. It's easy to understand how an extravagant mountain of presents makes it impossible for a child to appreciate the value and uniqueness of any one toy. By extension, we can see how easy, cheap access to fast food, music, Netflix, Buzzfeed, flat-screen TVs, washing machines and frankly incredible high quality free porn would desensitise us to more simple things we once appreciated. Our daily household chores now take minutes, and a half-hour trip to Blockbuster Video is now accomplished in the click of a button; maybe we have become spoiled. Still, I don't buy it as the whole story.

Another man of letters, Sir Aldous Huxley (he actually never made Sir, but let's pretend), described in his book Brave New World a civilization where all human desires are either satisfied, or suppressed through genetics and conditioning - there's abundant no-strings-attached sex, and a wealth of supersonic helicopters. When I read it for the first time I thought it was about the evils of technology, and how science was going to make us less and less equal. What I'd tell you if you asked me now is that it's actually about how removing the risk and struggle from our lives - and granting instant gratification - makes us less human. Bernard Marx - the 'hero' - is a freak and social outcast because he harbours frustrated desires for things that he shouldn't. Unlike the other satisfied folks in the book he is a neurotic human, and we relate to him because he is insecure and inadequate: he doesn't fit in, he can't get what he wants. Like Steinbeck's America, the horror of Huxley's utopia is that in negating our desires we have nothing to strive for to better ourselves. We have a questionable reason to exist at all.

The 'sickness of excess' is only part of the equation. By steadily automating the menial tasks in our lives (through microwave ovens and self-driving cars) we eliminate tasks that we once felt satisfied in performing as part of pursuing a different and better life. This gives us headspace and time to be occupied by other things, but unfortunately has taken away the need for many people to be employed - society's structure has not evolved to value and promote the activities that we find fulfilling, or which we feel provide meaning to us. Most accountants, software engineers and doctors receive salaries comparable to others in their field, but for our writers, artists, musicians, athletes and professional gamers, only a tiny minority generate enough money to live on. When traditional livelihoods are being eroded, what do the majority of people aspire to?

A 2012 UCLA study[1] found that the most popular future goal amongst a large sample of 10-12 year olds in America was being famous solely for the sake of being famous. It overshadowed hopes for financial success, achievement, or a sense of community. A further study[2] isolated "The desire to be seen/valued" as the primary reason for seeking fame. Very few people will be unfamiliar with shows like Pop Idol, The X Factor or Big Brother. These shows - the very definition of manufactured celebrity - are what many people perceive as their one shot at fame. Our short attention spans mean that we forget that the F-listers they churn out have an exceptionally short shelf-life, and that 99% of the 1% who 'make it' are dumped inside of 6 months. The fact that every other newspaper headline is some pop-star on a drug binge, and every other photo one of Miley Cyrus' or Nicki Minaj's or Kim Kardashian's ass, means that we still believe that celebrity - even for its own sake - is the shortest path to success.

It's easy to pursue what everyone else pursues - following received wisdom will not ruffle feathers or make us uncomfortable in the short term. In the long term, though, it will almost invariably leave us unfulfilled. Following the crowd means you are many times more likely to follow the path to a middle-of-the-road, obscure, grey, desk life, and this is a problem that affects us regardless of our

---

1   http://goo.gl/RZUPIR - The Value of Fame: Preadolescent Perceptions of Popular Media and Their Relationship to Future Aspirations (2011)
2   http://goo.gl/9gUQPc - Fame and the social self: The need to belong, narcissism, and relatedness predict the appeal of fame (2013

upbringing or intelligence. Speaking at a conference in Silicon Valley, Neal Stephenson famously noted of the PHDs and genius engineers he knew, "I saw the best minds of my generation...writing spam filters." Leaving university years ago, I watched some of the most unique, creative minds of my leaving class willfully step onto the conveyor belt into corporate law; investment banking; mergers and acquisitions - careers they were expected to take up, and which they grudgingly tolerated, or (eventually) abandoned, but which few ever enjoyed.

Each of us is unique in our passions, talents and desires, which statistically (thanks maths!) makes it exceptionally unlikely that a 'conventional' life will be the one you find satisfying.

Especially in a world where the unreal promise of celebrity and fame is always dangled above our heads, it becomes so much harder to experiment with what could make you happy, and to depart from the views of the crowd. The first step to everyone being able to choose a path in life with impunity, and without the prejudice of their peers, is letting go of the preconceived notions of one life being better than another. One thing may be better for you but - thankfully - no-one else in this world is you. This means you get to be unique, and everyone else does too. Since we were hunter-gatherers our gradually increasing quality of life, plus the automation of mundane tasks, has given us more time to think, more time to worry, and more time to spend pursuing the things we want. Unfortunately, when you take away the simple things, what's left is hard. Discovering a purpose, working out what you want to achieve, and working out the skills you need to do accomplish it are the hardest things we have to do with our lives. Peer pressure and the prevailing cult of celebrity are two devils on our shoulders - they are two unfortunate symptoms of our society that narrow our scope, and give us an easy, but misleading path to follow in the pursuit of happiness. They tell us that following what is Different is dangerous, unlikely to succeed; that others will look at us and sneer.

And then there's money.

In accelerating our modern lives - in trading and exchanging things - money is chief lubricant. Right about now you're maybe expecting me to break out the 'root of all evil' schtick, and tell you how the pursuit of money is the antithesis of difference, diversity and happiness. Well, you're only half right.
It's human nature to compare and to compete, and money is the common standard by which we can compare ourselves to others. It's hard to know whether the guy with ten houses is richer than the heiress with five yachts, but a peek at their 'net worth' in the Forbes list lets us think we know who is worth more.

Money is what allows us to get something we need. It's what allows us to exchange our hard work, or the things we own, for the things we can't make ourselves. In a world without money there would be much exchanging of sheep for bricks, or wood for wheat, but no standard price for anything, and it would be absurdly difficult to get hold of all the things we take for granted in our homes. Imagine a government trying to pull together the necessaries for a nuclear reactor based on a barter economy. How many chickens for that rod of plutonium?

Money is actually really useful.

The problem is that just as we get caught up aspiring to fame for fame's sake, we slip into the pursuit of money, rather than the experiences and happiness that we can use that money to gain. You think while you're growing up that you need money to be happy, and maybe you do, at least a bit, to be secure. And once you're making enough you kind of want to make more, because everyone you hang around with now makes just as much, or more, than you do, and you won't be happy until you have as much as them. We aspire to be rich rather than happy, and we fall into the trap of believing that a higher net worth is equivalent to a better standard of life.

Money is the means, not the end. You take a pile of money and you can turn it into almost anything; a family holiday, a wedding ring, or a home. You can use it to organise celebrations with friends, or to experience music and art. When money becomes the pursued thing - the goal - it's like watching the Big Bang in reverse. All of the millions of creative and diverse experiences we could use money to get become subsumed by the monolithic, dead idea of the money itself, as coins in a vault, or a string of numbers on a computer screen.

Unfortunately, no-one is telling us anything different. The insanely unaffordable New York loft apartments that twenty-somethings on TV shows live in make us feel bad about our $1500 a month box room. The chiseled, stubbly guy driving the Jaguar on the billboard looks younger than you, but he somehow managed to buy a $100,000 car. Advertising is one thing; it's explicit and it's loud. But the systems which gear us to pursue the money, and not the value it brings, are embedded far deeper in our psyches and our societies.

Just like the companies we work for, our countries need money to stay in business. They have to trade, pay the army, provide healthcare - it makes sense. Countries, though, are so large that they have to standardise things. We standardisie weights and measures, we standardise currency, and we standardise language. If you think about how nationalist propaganda is used to standardise values and beliefs (Maoism, The American Dream) it's not so great a leap to realise that a country can standardise the aspirations of its citizens. In fact, it can't really help itself.

In crafting our education systems, the range of things we are taught to aspire to is narrowed. For the longest time our children were encouraged to be doctors, or lawyers, or bankers, and now we are encouraging them to take up computer science. What has changed is the economic value of that job, rather than a belief that it provides a more spiritually fulfilling life, or will make us happier. A government doesn't care too much about the cars it produces, or the diamonds it digs out of the ground. It cares that they have value for trade, and that they can be used to sustain the income of money. And because many of our states undergo multi-party elections every few years, they unfortunately focus disproportionately on short-term gains, because short-term happiness is what will keep them in power at the next election. Having citizens who can make money is fundamentally important, because governments that don't have money stop being governments pretty quickly.

Unfortunately that means that from a very young age we are taught to pursue the thing that brings money, rather than the potential that money brings to us. It is a very conventional belief to have, and it is very unconventional to believe that opting out of the pursuit of wealth will likely result in happiness. Even in less profitable fields, like music, the arts, poetry, we still value most those who achieved fame and financial gain, rather than those who die obscure and unprosperous, but happy and fulfilled.

Money is probably the most flexible tool we have in getting the things that we want in life, but it is not fulfillment It is quite possible to be happy without money, and there is nothing you can buy with money that you can't somehow get without money. The money trap begins with looking at those around you. It is believing that to have a good life you have to be in competition with the accountant and the banker. The money trap is believing that net worth is happiness, and that that number at the bottom of your bank account is tallying your fulfillment. The money trap is an enemy to Difference because it slots you neatly into the job that maximises your money-making ability, but not the life that might make you happiest.

This book exists because of Difference. It exists because healthy, beautiful ecosystems thrive on diversity, and the ones that are not diverse become stagnant and xenophobic. It exists because we should all be allowed to think and live differently, to aspire to an experience of Difference as broad as the menagerie of species on our planet, and to not face prejudice or repression when we do so. It exists because the world we live in impairs this freedom.

It exists because Difference is a fundamental part of our condition. Although we like to believe in a universe of dualism - of good and evil, order and chaos, Batman and the Joker - what we have is at best a spectrum, and at worst a mess. We have up quarks and down quarks but also charm quarks. Protons and neutrons, electrons and positrons, neutrinos and gravitons and, deep down, an unpredictable quantum foam where 1 could be 0 or anything in between. We have fifty shades of democracy but no system that is truly democratic, capitalists in China performing a masquerade of communism. Everything is different from everything else, and nothing is the same. And that is why pigeon-holing ideas can sometimes be helpful - just to make sense of the chaos - but to pigeon-hole a person is to take a liberty with their lives.

Silver bullets

At the end of the acclaimed graphic novel Watchmen a Machiavellian genius has forged a new world peace between the USA and the USSR. As he goes to his chamber to meditate, he remarks to his friend that everything "worked out in the end". Leaving the room, his friend reminds him "Nothing ends, Adrian. Nothing ever ends."

Like the uneasy peace at the end of Watchmen, human happiness, satisfaction and fulfillment can only ever be ephemeral. Not only is there no silver bullet for making everyone happy, but ambition and competition - wanting things which are better than we had before - are core, genetically coded parts of human nature. We got where we are as a species by competing with other animals, by wanting what they have, or by being the best of the bunch, and we're rarely satisfied with what we have, and never for long. That's why a multi-millionaire pop star can have a supermodel wife, a beach house in Santa Monica and legions of adoring fans, but still turn to drugs in depression. We reset our expectations every time things get better, and expect more and more. To take this away is to take away the essence of what makes us human.

There is a strange symmetry - a seductive semblance of dualism - in exploring our universe's relationship with our own humanity. As it grows from the Big Bang our universe expands into difference and disorder, and yet we believe its chaotic growth will end in a 'thermal equilibrium'. At the end of aeons of growth, we believe that the ultimate displacement and disorder will lead to a completely even, ordered distribution of matter and energy. Likewise, as human beings we have evolved to be restless, competitive and dissatisfied; striving and irregularly expanding in search of what is different and new. And yet, the more we discover and disrupt, the more we categorise and taxonomise. We intervene and impose order. We legislate and build surveillance, prescribe algorithms to control our traffic lights and sleep patterns, fill our mobile phones with sensors designed to track our location and surroundings. We relentlessly seek to rationalise the behaviour of 7 billion separate organisms.

Everywhere we look we observe balance. We see it everywhere from the precarious ecosystems in a tide pool to the silent orbit of our planets around their sun. We create it for ourselves in our stories - the balance between good and evil - and we worship it in our star signs and mythologies. From a distance, in a snapshot, all is serene and still. Close up, against the moving backdrop of time, it is a mess, a scramble, a turf war.

Happiness isn't the same for all of us, and it isn't the same for any one of us over time. What I want now will probably change once I have my first child, or my first grandchild, or my third wife.

The mantra of this book is that we as individuals are the balance and difference - we are the counterweight to the ossifying order of the establishment. Against systems which by their nature create bureaucracy and sameness it is our duty - almost our destiny - to do anything and everything we can to be not only agents of change, but to help create a world where fulfillment and happiness are recognised not as uniform, attainable ideals, but as fireflies jumping out of the hand as soon as they are caught. Aspirations are unique to each one of us, and are unique to their time.

What is to be done

Each of the three central sections in this book is an experiment. It asks you to entertain something you might not agree with and, by looking at the world and countries we live in, to test whether things could be better with this way of thinking. The final section is a bestiary of sorts, a collection of practical and radical things that people are doing right now to try and live differently, or to help others to embrace Difference. It's there to show you that some pretty amazing things are happening right now, and that many others are not just possible, but in many ways inevitable.

Each chapter is modeled loosely around one of three fundamental things that our biggest social systems need in order to function, but which risk crushing our individuality and desires if they are unchecked. The first is **Difference of thought**, why we need nonconformism in society to challenge the big systems that surround us and impose order and standardisation. The second is **Difference of identity**, the way in which those thick straight lines on maps demarcate not only our national boundaries, but also who we are and who we are not. And the third is **Difference of perspective** or, more specifically, how right and wrong are not absolutes, but fluid and evolving definitions within our countries.

Put simply, Difference is. It's a common aphorism in this ever-expanding universe that the only constant is change, but it's an appropriate one. Embracing it allows us to stay happy, and as a society we neglect diversity of thought and opinion at our peril.

Studies are inconclusive as to whether there's a salary "plateau" after which we stop feeling happier or more satisfied with our lives, but it doesn't take a rocket surgeon to realise that the pursuit of material goals (designer clothes, a fast car, a preponderance of bling) might not be the long term key to making us happy. Knowing that our desires and circumstances will change, the question we have to ask ourselves should not be "what do I want to be satisfied right now?", but rather "what should I aspire to be in future, that is most likely to make me happy"?.

An organism is the sum of its millions of teeming constituent parts. You are the 5 people closest to you, but you are also your parent's education, your first breakup, that unfortunate night in the drunk tank. We're not nihilists. Unlike Nietzsche, we're not beyond good and evil; we're beyond one good and one evil; we're a recognition that there are 7 billion different pantone colour swatches of what's good and what's evil, and that these 7 billion are what make up the world. The way to embrace Difference is to embrace a system that thrives on Difference and whose first reaction is to flex and accommodate it, rather than stamping it out in place of artificial uniformity. It makes us stronger, smarter, brighter, freer. If there is to be a scale on which our systems are weighed, we are the 7 billion fingers tipping it in favour of Difference.

In praise of being Different

Be a nonconformist, and support the actions of nonconformists. To conform is to become part of a structure that compels others to conform.

Once upon a time there were two mice; cousins who as they grew up had gone their separate ways in life. One mouse lived in the city, and one lived in the countryside. One day, the country mouse invited his cousin to stay with him. The city mouse arrived, and though he received nuts and raisins to eat, and a warm bed to sleep in, he was unhappy. The old country house creaked and moved with the wind in the night, and his cousin woke him at sunrise to forage in the field. By the following evening - when it was time to go - he was exhausted; country life was not for him. As he left, he invited his cousin back to the city, where the city mouse knew his cousin would appreciate the finer food and modern conveniences of urban living.

The country mouse traveled far to visit his cousin in the city, and when he arrived his cousin had laid out a feast: he had cakes and jellies from his master's pantry, and the light from the master's candle meant they could talk long into the night. The country mouse was grateful for his cousin's hospitality, but the rich food upset his stomach, and the noise of traffic and the hubbub from the streets kept him awake all night. In the morning, tired and still nursing a stomach ache, he waved goodbye to his cousin in the city, vowing to never return.

As children we are told the fable of the town mouse and the country mouse. What it teaches us - other than the fact that mice are really damn picky (who knew?) - is that different people like different things. It's a sentiment echoed in aphorisms across the world, from the English "one man's meat is another man's poison" to the slightly more esoteric Ghanaian "You can't force a baboon to eat tamarind fruits" (that's a real aphorism, look it up!). It teaches us that what makes us happy might very well make someone else miserable. It teaches us that people are different, and that we shouldn't presume that we know what is best for others.

Equality is a hot topic these days. We are told every day that we live in a world where the rich are getting richer and the poor are getting poorer. It's not a new problem, but across the world it has been a cyclical one. Karl Marx, the father of communist thought, sought to counter this trend in 1875 with a novel approach to society that you may have heard before:

From each according to his ability, to each according to his need.

The echo of this phrase is present today in books like The Spirit Level (by Richard Wilkinson and Kate Pickett). Their prevailing sentiment is that "equality is better for everyone" and that a society with reduced wealth disparity is - overall - happier, healthier and plagued less by crime. And it's hard to argue that a society, at the very least where people started off with the same chances, would be less fair than what we have right now in countries like the UK or the US.

Unfortunately there's a difference between equalising 'wealth', and creating a world where everyone is happy. To 'solve' society by making everyone equal is - like our town mouse and country mouse - to assume that what everyone wants is the same. It's a shallow way of thinking about happiness. Appreciating that everyone wants different things helps us realise that the best way to work towards the happiness and fulfillment of a large group of unique people is to give them the best possible opportunity to learn and grow; to discover what they want and to pursue it. Having as our first principle the creation of opportunity, rather than trying to retroactively render people 'equal', helps us to encourage diversity rather than conformity. It helps us to think about things, people and their lives as inherently different rather than inherently better than one another.

Like our mice, we know that people want different things. From experience, we also know that people value things differently and, more than this, that external circumstances - like where you live, or who you're surrounded by - will make us value things differently. If I live in a built-up city with great public transport but congested roads, I might not take a car off you if you were giving it away, let alone if you wanted me to pay for it. Where would I put it? I'd have to pay for parking, for road tax, for repairs, and I probably wouldn't even use it that much; what a nightmare! If I lived in the Scottish highlands, though, I'd need a car just for the 30 minute drive to the supermarket. Given all the space out there, I'd also probably have a garage, or a drive (or a few spare fields) to put it on.

If we wanted to make everyone equal, should everyone get one car, even though it's actually a burden to some? If I don't get a car and someone else does, can we be equal? The 'equality' many strive for is an economic model of GDP per capita, rather than a practical possibility. If we can agree that giving a lump sum of $1000 to two people from different backgrounds (say a prince and a pauper) would not give them the same amount of happiness, we can begin to see how standardising happiness through material assets is fundamentally impossible. People want different things, and different things have different values to different people.

And happiness neither is nor should be a purely material concern. Some people really want children, and would get the same level of happiness from raising a child as another person might get from having a pilot's licence. Trying to make people equal means you have to have a proxy; a common item that helps you compare people (so far it has tended to be money). But we're social animals, and can't help but judge our own happiness based on the lives of those around us. Happiness based on income is relative to the income of everyone around you. If you're living in San Francisco and your neighbours are twenty-something tech entrepreneurs with millions in the bank, you're unfortunately less likely to feel personally satisfied than if you live up the coast in Portland, Oregon, where something of an alternative counterculture still thrives. Money can be a proxy for estimating quality of life, but it is not a tool that can be used to arbitrarily influence it.

Relativity

In 2007 Prof Christian Elger and Prof Armin Falk at the University of Bonn tested men in pairs, asking them to perform the simple task of counting dots on a screen. They promised payment for success. The researchers studied the brain activity of 38 men as they played the games, side by side. If they had solved the task correctly, they received a reward, which might range from 30 to 120 Euros. Each participant also learnt how his partner in the game had performed, and how much money his partner would pocket. Players felt most satisfied in situations where they got the right answer but their partner got it wrong. Participants who got more money than their partners also showed much stronger activation in the 'reward centre' of the brain than when both received the same amount. Happiness with a material reward like money is closely related to the success of those around you. These men were motivated by money, but their happiness was actually more predicated on relative success than simply the amount they took home.

So, where do we go from here? In a world where happiness is different for everyone, and where we know that satisfaction is relative, and only temporary (pretty soon we're going to want a new job, or kids, or to pack it all in and live on a farm), how do we judge the success of our societies, and how do we create communities that can be flexible enough to accommodate a potentially huge diversity of evolving desires?

First (as problematic as it is) we recognise that the fundamental engine for our happiness is Difference. The ephemeral satisfaction that we get in our lives comes from achievement and fulfillment, but this is only possible because things change, and there is always something new and different to aspire to. Being spoon-fed the same life day by day makes us miserable and, like Huxley's Brave New World, if nothing changes, nothing can really be good or bad. We acknowledge this, and then we channel a quotation often (wrongly - Google it!) attributed to Voltaire:

I disapprove of what you say, but I will defend to the death your right to say it.[3]

We remind ourselves that as a society talking about things is infinitely preferable to fighting about them, and that if we don't allow people to express what they think and believe in a safe public space - and debate it with them - that they are many times more likely to break from mainstream society, cultivate extreme ideologies, and return with acts of violence or aggression. This happened in the UK's treatment of Ireland, and it is happening today amongst violent fundamentalist religious groups. Free forums for discourse allow us to debunk lies (engaging holocaust

---

3   [3]Evelyn Beatrice Hall writing under the pseudonym of Stephen G Tallentyre in The Friends of Voltaire (1906)

deniers allows them to demonstrate the fallacy of their own beliefs) whereas suppressing minority viewpoints narrows our own perspective, and makes it likely that those marginalised will resort to other methods (think of Fathers4Justice occupying landmarks in the UK, or Chechen separatists rebelling in Russia). Constraining discourse drives a wedge between different groups of society, and places each side of the argument in an echo chamber, convinced of their own self-righteousness. There is no acknowledgement of Difference (rather than right or wrong), and no common ground.

Even if a viewpoint seems illogical, stupid, or morally repulsive to us, we should not deny its expression. No-one can always be correct, and whatever humility we have should allow us to realise that our own thoughts can often be wrong or based on false assumptions. Having a diversity of opinions - rationally explored - is the only way to make informed conclusions. The approach of illegalising what are perceived as 'extreme views' leads to narrow-mindedness, the restriction of our ability to change and, eventually, despotism. Those who argued against slavery, racism, equal rights for women and the legalisation of homosexuality were at one point considered radicals, but the vast majority of us consider ourselves lucky that they eventually found somewhere to air their views.

Unreasonable Men

Radical thoughts come from individuals or small groups on the ideological fringes of society. If they came from the majority then they wouldn't be radical. George Bernard

Shaw, in 'Maxims for Revolutionists', frames it this way:

The reasonable man adapts himself to the world; the unreasonable one persists in trying to adapt the world to himself. Therefore all progress depends on the unreasonable man.[4]

Shaw's 'unreasonable man' is not necessarily a revolutionary. He becomes disruptive and challenging because the world he lives in is one which is unwilling to let him explore or realise his vision. If it won't accommodate him, his only recourse is to rebel. The first problem is that traditional big systems rely on orthodoxy; they can only function if everyone is pulling in the same direction with the same beliefs. Order and stability are required, whereas Difference represents risk (and not opportunity). A larger problem is that authorities force reformers like Shaw's to be defined by society as 'unreasonable' if they want to change something; there is a baseline understanding that what is different is deviant, and the instinct is to suppress rather than to experiment.

The true tragedy, though, is that the world is populated by billions of men and women who are 'reasonable' only because they are not able to break the orthodoxy into which they are born. Many people harbour divergent views and aspirations, but suppress them either because they fear ridicule by peers, reprisal (like violent suppression or the 'disappearing' of friends and family), or simply failure.

---

4   George Bernard Shaw, 'Maxims for Revolutionists' in Man and Superman, 1903 (via Kurzweil)

The difference between 'reasonable' and 'unreasonable' is one made by society at large, generally by government and media. Shaw's usage indicates how large, established bodies mistake nonconformism for "unreasonableness"; again something opposed to convention which is to be treated with caution, rather than curiosity. But really no-one 'aspires' to nonconformism, they just find their own desires at odds with the status quo. In the world we live in the 'unreasonable man' is not just suppressed; many of our most radical, celebrated thinkers (Galileo, Mandela, Ai Weiwei) were imprisoned and persecuted for years for vocalising or acting on their nonconformist tendencies.

Like the birth of a new star, a radically different perspective can create things - it can bring heat, warmth and new life. But it can also disrupt and destroy. The motorcar revolutionised transportation and travel - it allowed families a hitherto unimaginable freedom and mobility - but it also caused noise, pollution, sprawling American suburbia and over a million deaths a year through accidents. Although they carry risk, radical and new ideas are integral to human happiness; providing new experiences and better living standards. On a galactic level, zooming out from that one new star shows us a living galaxy whose evolution and growth depends on the birth, death and recycling of whole solar systems. Likewise, our collective existence is built on adapting to change. Everything disrupts something, but when we experiment on a small scale we maximise the opportunity in difference, and mitigate the potentially harmful effects.

Unfortunately, the systems and governments within which

our countries operate are not set up to allow experimentation. Top-down structures mean they are poorly equipped to manage difference - orders come from the top, rather than experiments being allowed to happen around the edges, where people have the most local knowledge and experience, and can report back to the centre. They spend decades ploughing money into narrow sectors of the financial services, and balk when markets crash and abandoned industries lie derelict. Rather than accommodating and growing through change they compete with it, and eventually respond against it.

If - like Assad in Syria - a system can suppress any desire for change, the status quo will prevail, and people will be oppressed. Alternatively, if it cannot contain the desire for change - like in the case of Egypt and the Tahrir Square protests - the system will collapse like a house of cards, leaving a dangerous power vacuum. Neither of these are what a society of people need to live secure and fulfilled lives. It is a shame, in that it is something of which we should be ashamed. In the same way as our slide into the grey, cubicled mundane seems opposed to our nature as the product of a teeming, infinitely diverse universe, it is paradoxical that our culture - which thrives on the new - will only tolerate so much independent thought.

Hero worship

The art world provides perhaps the clearest illustration of where, as a society, we believe creativity and innovation come from. The heroes we praise are individuals, and not institutions. Leonardo da Vinci, or Shakespeare, or Mozart are the figures that come to our minds, and it's rare that we would name a nation or a ruling political party as being the agent of change, although we do sometimes pick movements, or a small cluster of individuals.

In the past religious bodies and wealthy benefactors commissioned the greatest art, and it would not exist without their patronage. Nevertheless, we invariably care about the creator of that art, and the creator is praised for technical skill. You could argue that the business acumen of the benefactor was instrumental in the art being created, but what we value above all else is the difference in perspective that the artist brought to what they created. Change in this field comes from minority groups at the fringes, those who experiment, rather than the masses who seek to perfect or reproduce an established medium. Consider conceptual or abstract art today; pieces like Damien Hirst's animals in formaldehyde, or Mondrian's abstract geometric compositions. Most of us have the technical skill capable to reproduce this art, but the act of making it first - being the individual to present a different take – is what gives it value. The modern conceptual artist's retort to the complaint "Anyone could do that if they wanted to," is, rightly, "But they didn't, did they?"

Even for art which genuinely was produced by a group or collective, praise is typically given to the 'visionary'; the one person who originated the idea. Andy Warhol's factory, and the disproportionate praise given to him rather than the artists who physically produced much of his work, is a good example of this. Other names that spring to mind are Monet (Impressionism), Picasso (Cubism), Dali

(Surrealism); individuals who were part of a movement – a group of larger people - but who were in many ways the figureheads; those who strove to do something different, and changed our approach to and appreciation of art. Likewise, in literature it is not a committee, group or state that is praised for great literature, but individual figures like, Milton, Eliot, Joyce, Nabokov. Methods for committee, or machine-made art - those depicted in fictional books like 1984 - are treated with disgust and a slow dread. As human beings we don't want art made by a system.

People will rarely tell you that they went to a great MGM, or Scott Free, or New Line film at the cinema. Likewise, we don't talk about that great new album released by Parlophone Records, or EMI. The smaller the publisher or organisation, the more of a cache it has (independent labels like RoughTrade are a good example), but people still attach more value to what they see as the origin-point - usually an individual - responsible for the creation; figures like Elvis Presley, or Michael Jackson, or Amy Winehouse. Music bands are a valid exception. There are thousands of examples of bands that we esteem, but even so individual leaders emerge, and they will be the ones credited with the most skill or creativity. Lennon & McCartney, Bono, the ginger one from the Spice Girls. You might be able to name Axl Rose and Slash out of Guns 'n' Roses, but can you name anyone else? What about the members of Muse other than Matt Bellamy, what about members of Police other than Sting, members of The Culture Club other than Boy George? I think that's probably enough.

There is a strong bias towards the individual in art. This

isn't because the idea for all great art is conceived and executed by individuals. Rather, the bias exists because in the system we live in it is easier for an individual to act on ideas that are nonconformist and different to the norm, and the more we take things to a committee or a board for approval, the more their uniqueness becomes diluted.

In Science & Technology, too, individuals prevail. Nations, companies and organisations pour billions into research and development, but still we mostly praise the individuals who were funded. The Curies, Pasteur, Einstein, Edison, Newton, Tesla, Hawking; our greatest scientific breakthroughs are in general attributed to individuals, and not groups, universities or countries. In politics, the names we can remember - for better or worse - are Plato, Socrates, Lenin, Marx, Churchill, Thatcher, Castro, Che Guevara; those who brought about a different way of doing things. Will people in the UK remember Iain Duncan Smith in thirty years? Some people probably don't even remember him now.

In multinational business, where large, faceless corporations are par for the course, there is a similar trend developing. Where there is disruption and change, it is associated with an individual; there is an architect. Facebook is Mark Zuckerberg, Apple is Steve Jobs, Virgin is Richard Branson. Can you name the CEO of Gillette? What about Microsoft? Years ago, when the company was new and innovative, it would have been Bill Gates, but what about now, now that the business is large, established, multinational, more slow-moving, more part of the establishment and less disruptive.

In general, we find that areas where we praise the work of the individual are the areas where drastic, disruptive or fast change to the established order takes place - new styles of art, or perspectives on the world; revolutionary new technologies or scientific models. New, desirable products (Jobs and the iPad), or the fast commercialisation of existing ones (Ford and the Model T) are those that capture the imagination. As an idea becomes accepted, or becomes mainstream, our attachment to the individuals who use it, practice it or sell it becomes diminished and more generalised. We may respect the technology, but we no longer revere our train builders as individual figures, or even those who build our space shuttles. The universe is one vast, ungoverned system, where the smallest change is a function of the largest, and vice versa. And as part of the universe, we are a function in that equation. As thinking, self-conscious humans, though, it is our nature to assign meaning to the changes that happen; some semblance of reason and order. It is only natural that we would look to ourselves.

Nonconformism is the trait celebrated most highly in many of history's preeminent artists, inventors and thinkers (Einstein, Tesla, Gaudi, Jobs), and it's often through this nonconformism that we identify their genius; a kind of eccentricity or mania. Uncoincidentally, it is the trait popularised by Jobs' Apple in its "Think Different" campaign:

The People who are crazy enough to think they can change the world, are the ones who do.

Jobs here is not too different to George Bernard Shaw, writing at the other end of the century, and it's not so surprising that one nonconformist can identify with another. What it indicates, though, is that a passion for difference can be a unifying force amongst a community, rather than just a disruptive force.

And this is because innovation doesn't happen in a vacuum. Difference thrives when we're surrounded by different people - ideas that do not conform - and difference in reality is not a pathway of individual genius buds, but the intermittent flowering of several patches of ideas, and even more rarely a blossoming of thousands. The Renaissance, for example, was a confluence of myriad ideas from the arts and sciences that brought together a cluster of great artists, and generated technological concepts - like Da Vinci's blueprint for a helicopter - hundreds of years ahead of their time. Likewise, the Age of Enlightenment brought together thinkers from across the disciplines of politics, religion, the arts and sciences in the pursuit of reason and a burgeoning scientific method.

Modern examples have come in the innovation that happens when several disparate technologies converge, or when parallel advances are made in different fields. The Internet, for example, was born out of Tim Berners-Lee and the combination of hypertext and the TCP protocol. It was born out of Vint Cerf, who pioneered the first commercial email. It would have been impossible without a pre-existing telecommunications infrastructure, and it provided a platform for hitherto impossible forms of communication tools. The Internet is a very different beast to what it was 20 years ago; now a platform for video, commerce, gaming; a means to turn on your hi-fi or phone your girlfriend. It exists in its current form because of the work of hardware manufacturers, software developers, telecommunications companies, cable companies and a host of other players; millions of individual people.

The way humanity initiates and responds to change seems invariably tied to the idea that small groups are responsible for a disproportionate amount of change. In the Arts, sciences, systems of politics and the realm of business we value pivotal individuals for the inception of the ideas that generate that change. It makes more sense in our minds to focus on the actions of a few, because it is so incalculably complex to trace the large-scale social trends that bring about a perfect storm of creativity. There is a spectrum that ranges from the high level and ungoverned social change that sweeps across societies, to the actions of a few pivotal instigators that catalyse them. In between, it is the man-made systems - committees, governments - that have tended to preserve the status quo and order of the past, when they should be recognising these overarching trends, fostering the talent of the avant-garde and - instead of bottling up resistance until we reach flashpoints like the French revolution or the Arab Spring - make sure to caretake the continual transition of society, as change inevitably takes place.

Free Radicals

History teaches us that nonconformism is essential to progress and enlightenment, and that we should aspire to use unique ideas to change society for the better. Unfortunately, we are increasingly told that the 'radical' and the 'extreme' are dangerous to the maintenance of order, and by extension to the stability of our happiness. Galileo's discovery that the earth moved around the sun, for example, challenged the orthodoxy of the church. He was branded a heretic and locked up in prison until he recanted his belief, and yet his work revolutionised astronomy, travel, and our understanding of the universe.

These individuals and groups challenge systems of order; those enforced by state governments or religious bodies. They represent a threat to power, and their ideas give them a disproportionate ability to 'change the game', to threaten established geographical borders and to threaten the way a state enforces the law. Ultimately, they alter the means by which people learn and get what they want, and marginalise broader authority. Think about developments in the last 20 years, and how file-sharing, globalised media, decentralised currencies (Bitcoin), Wikileaks and Edward Snowden, online gambling and ecommerce have jeopardised our systems' control over taxation, education, state secrets and international news. Think about V for Vendetta by Alan Moore, which is 'just a book', and yet has given a face and figurehead to a global protest movement, and which challenges government from behind the eyes of one million anonymous Guy Fawkes masks.

As living, sentient creatures we are unique. The rest of our observable universe does not concern itself with managing or preventing change. Its nature is change, and every reaction and collision - every solar flare and asteroid collision - combines in its inevitable expansion and evolution. As people, though, we need to justify change; understand it and its effects before we are comfortable with letting them take their course. Just as no-one tries to stop the world turning or the stars shining, we should know that resisting 'change' in its purest sense is a losing battle. We would be far better positioned to benefit from change, and mitigate the disruption that it causes, by having luminaries leading our communities who embrace difference; people who anticipate the inevitable trends, and who maximise the benefit that change will bring. How much further along would we be as a society if we had recognised the groundswell of support for women's rights, or homosexuality? How many more lives and deaths will have to be dedicated to combating institutional racism? Think how much the energy and passion of those people - that love of diversity - could have accomplished elsewhere if the establishment had not solidified against it and battled with progress for hundreds of years. If it had instead seen, embraced and been participant in reform before a single placard had to be raised or a march marched; if the system could be a collaborator rather than a rival; if the system and the difference of its constituent parts (that's us!) could be one.

Where states and governments do praise inventors, artists and innovators, it is generally in retrospect. Martin Luther King day in the US is a memorial when it should have been a monument to someone living, brilliant and alive. Our system praises change that has been popular and conventional. It praises difference only when it has almost ceased to be different. At the moment it seems that our systems of authority cannot help but suppress difference at the expense of stability. But there is an alternative to the state that guts people's individualism, and which teaches them to want the same things as each other; a model in which individuality can be celebrated at its inception, and where the radicalism and innovation that it engenders can be exploited without the systemic societal disruption that comes from our revolutions and chronic social unrest.

Countries hire ministers for innovation in the same breath as placing absurd restrictions on businesses (salut France, who banned the free delivery of books to hinder Amazon's ecommerce efforts). Most Western democracies also claim to support freedom of speech and radical free-thinking. A free press, and freedom to talk openly on any topic at Hyde Park Corner are iconic symbols of free speech in the UK. Municipal monuments and buildings in France are also adorned with references to the state's revolutionary past. "Live free or die", and "Liberty, Equality, Fraternity" are common mantras. America, too, has freedom of speech enshrined in its constitution, and the government endorses the famous rights to "life, liberty and the pursuit of happiness."

But with the spectres of Guantanamo Bay, and international complicity with 'black sites' where detainees are taken to be horrifically tortured[5] hanging over these

---

5   http://goo.gl/ShO9QO - Slate: The Most Gruesome Moments in the CIA 'Torture Report' (2014)

countries, you have to wonder whether it is actually upheld in practice. Is our system of government geared towards protecting and allowing truly free and open discourse, and all that it entails (a free press, free expression etc.) or is free speech just the freedom to say what other people want to hear?

Some biases are unfounded, but let's be mature when we talk about treating people differently. Inconvenient truth though it may be, people are different, on some fundamental levels. Women, in general, are not as physically strong as men (which is why we don't have mixed-gender olympic events). Men can't (at least right now) naturally carry and give birth to children. Asian people tend to be shorter than Europeans, and so on. Sexism, racism and the other -isms are damaging, but no-one is created equal, and some differences are quantifiable. With that out of the way, many discriminations are made which have no grounding in science. If I believed and said, for example, that Swedish people are innately more stupid than English people, or that men are naturally worse at playing the trombone than women, I would have a hard time backing it up with facts. It is not uncommon, even in what most people would call "developed" countries, to hear men say women can't read maps, or to hear black people say that white people can't play basketball, and these things don't bear up to analysis.

In its purest form, almost no society tolerates completely free speech. You can't just stand on a street corner telling passers-by that black people are evil and that they should all be killed. You would be stopped, either by the police or by passers-by, harassed and probably assaulted by people that you'd offended. In either case, freedom of speech is limited and informally policed by the prejudices and beliefs of those around you. You just can't say anything you want anywhere you want.

Countries like the UK do allow a more socially accepted 'free speech', though. TV shows like Newsnight provide a forum for political debate, and those with radical views - like onetime British National Party leader Nick Griffin - have in the past been allowed to express their views, and have them criticised.

When your viewpoint challenges authority rather than a minority group, things become more restrictive far more quickly. Myself, the press, and political parties are not (explicitly or legally) restricted from expressing opinions for and against other political parties. In fact, it is a hallmark of democracy that this scrutiny is allowed. Again, though, a forum for this debate is necessary, and anti-government is very different to anti-state. Plenty of publications in the UK, for example, openly criticise the incumbent government for corruption or incompetency, but very few criticise the idea of the state, or the idea of the current structure of government that exists in the UK. They may say that the government is acting in an undemocratic way, but no established publication has seriously questioned the idea of the state as it exists in the UK. If one of us openly said that we wanted to remove the current state system and replace it, and promoted this view in an organised way, we would be arrested as terrorists, or for inciting terrorism. Back in the day this was called 'sedition', and people were hanged for it - a threat to established order trumps a government's willingness to entertain free speech.

Think about Abu Hamza al-Masri; the Egyptian Sunni activist. Many find his views distasteful, and do not condone the practices he preaches, but if we believe in free speech he should have the right to vocalise them. In 2006 he was convicted of soliciting murder and of "using threatening, abusive or insulting words or behaviour with the intention of stirring up racial hatred". Interestingly, he was also convicted for the possession of recordings related to "stirring up racial hatred, and of possessing a "terrorist encyclopaedia" (under the Terrorism Act 2000, s58). It is easy to see why a government would want to imprison an individual who was stirring up disorder and violence, but interesting to see that just owning a 'recording' and a 'terrorist encyclopaedia' are criminal offences. Expressing a viewpoint, as well as owning a record of someone else's views, can be an illegal act. Some books are banned.

The case of Abu Hamza is extreme, and he is an extreme individual, but the surveillance and suppression of individuals with 'radical', anti-state viewpoints is carried out openly in the UK. In 2011 the Guardian Newspaper[6] reported on the Westminster police department, and how they openly requested that people report 'anarchist' neighbours or acquaintances to the police. The justification for this mobilisation against a minority political group was as follows:

---

6   http://goo.gl/4FJNKn - Guardian: Anarchists should be reported, advises Westminster anti-terror police (2011)

Anarchism is a political philosophy which considers the state undesirable, unnecessary, and harmful, and instead promotes a stateless society, or anarchy. Any information relating to anarchists should be reported to your local police.

Although not a criminal act in and of itself, and not stated as such, holding these beliefs was used as a justification by the police department to keep a watch on them. Even in situations where it is not explicitly legislated against, anti-statism is treated as 'dangerous' and inherently 'bad'; political moralising is used to fudge the boundaries of the law, in a similar way to the 'public shaming' of big companies that took place to get them to pay more taxes, even though they had broken no law. The moral beliefs, or professed beliefs, of a few individuals in power is not a good basis for legislation. Better to have governance be a synthesis of the views of its people - a network which is receptive to the pockets of difference within it, and how they influence one another - rather than a monolithic centre; a few biased individuals who enforce at best a dated generalization of its citizens' desires, and at worse a distant, elitist agenda.

Decidophobia

Back to Shaw's 'unreasonable man' for a moment. In the short term, it's easier to see when radical thinkers are ostracised or punished - they get put in prison, like Nelson Mandela, or assassinated, like Malcolm X, or persecuted, like Gandhi. What's harder to measure, and on a larger scale far more damaging to human happiness, is the suppression of 'reasonable' men and women, who still think differently, and want things to be different, but feel unable to act; part of a system they cannot change. These are the silent majority siphoned off into cubicles; put on a slow train to breakdowns, midlife crises or just obscurity.

And the disenfranchisement of 'reasonable' people is part of the reason that a desire for money and fame becomes so pervasive. Not only have we been educated (formally and through advertising and media) to believe that it's what we should aspire to, but actually deciding what you should do with your life is really hard. All of us are plagued at one point or another by Decidophobia™ - the fear that making a big life change is far more risky than following the status quo. We'd much rather follow a seemingly well-trodden sensible direction, than have to pick the best one for ourselves and risk failure. Getting more money seems like it will help us be happy; it seems sensible until we hit 60 and realise that we never actually spent any of our life doing something fulfilling.

Living life is pretty difficult. We have to find jobs, raise kids, pay taxes, pay rent, do the shopping, fetch our kids from school, pay our mortgage, get home insurance, and it goes on. We make so many thousands of decisions on a daily basis that it's exhausting; do I want full-fat milk; should I take the highway; what do I want for lunch; how can I ask for a raise without seeming greedy; what time do I need to be back this evening to pick up the kids from school; I wonder if I should ask that girl out? The amount of things we have to juggle and decide upon from minute to minute is mind-boggling and exhausting, and a growing body of research[7] indicates that we expend mental effort with every decision we make, and that hinders our ability to make others throughout the day.

It's why Barack Obama only wears blue or grey suits[8], and it's why programmed television was so successful - people didn't want to have to decide what to watch after a long day at work, they wanted to be told. At the extreme end, it's also why restaurants no longer have bible-sized menus, just a few select items. People are exhausted by the choice, and want to trust in someone to curate the best choices for them.

It's also why we often let someone else decide things for us; be it a colleague, a barista, a traffic warden or the government. Life is exhausting enough without having to work out the details of the Common Agricultural Policy. These things are hard to care about in the moment, and the slew of decisions we have to make often leave us happy to have someone else decide for us. A government is comprised of 'public servants' who are supposed to make these decisions, with our best interests as human beings in mind. Some are publicly elected, but the majority are not. They are supposed to be experts in the issues we don't have time to be experts on, and we rely on them to make decisions about our healthcare, salaries and taxes. I

---

7   http://goo.gl/Mpp5FQ - Scientific American: Tough Choices: How Making Decisions Tires Your Brain (2008)
8   http://goo.gl/TFcayH - Lifehacker: President Obama's Productivity Tactics (2012)

haven't done the research myself, but I think I can make a good estimate (at least in my home country of the UK) as to whether 'public servants' with 'our best interests in mind' is the way in which most people would describe their government. CassetteBoy's Cameron Rap[9], with 4 million views on youtube in one month, and overwhelming support from the people who watched it, I think answers it better than I could myself.

Being part of a large organization, or a small part of a big system, narrows our perspective, and suppresses our individuality. But legislation and government pressure is also pro-active. It has been used to repress socialists (the McCarthy witch-hunts in America), ethnic minorities (those persecuted in NAZI Germany), religious minorities (like the Baha'i in Iran), or homosexuals (imprisoning Oscar Wilde or chemically castrating Alan Turing); the list is global and without end. These things did not happen because of government, but because of the way the government was set up - a small group with centralised and absolute control over power and enforcement, who could very easily suppress radical and challenging ideas.

Is this suppression of individualism and Difference deliberate? Is it a sinister and intentional move by a state to secure its own authority? In some cases, like the request by Westminster police to report on 'the anarchist next door'[10], the answer is yes. In other cases, though,

---

9   http://goo.gl/G2CORw - Cameron's Conference Rap (2014)

10   http://goo.gl/4FJNKn - Guardian: Anarchists should be

things are not so clear cut. In a book called Boundaries of Order, Butler Shaffer offers an opinion on how these tactics manifest in the education system:

They [children] are compelled, by law, to attend schools that look and function like penitentiaries where they are subjected to often mindless curricula that have no apparent meaning to their lives. Those who exhibit any independence in the classroom are labeled "hyperactive" or victims of "attention deficit disorder" - meaning they have their own agendas that differ from the teachers - and are legally drugged into more compliant behaviour.[11]

His view, that schools are tools for brainwashing and enforcing conformity, is extreme. Curriculum and discipline almost by definition encourage uniformity of thought and action, but this is not always the principle on which they are run. School education in the UK, the US, and most other countries, is still geared towards priming students with the tools they need to be successful and valuable. In these countries governments are acutely aware that creativity and technological innovation are the means by which their countries will survive in the 21st century.

Unfortunately, though, in delivering the 'basics' of education in large classes that cover a wide spectrum of abilities, education tends towards a middle ground, and encourages one way of thinking, and one approach to

---

reported, advises Westminster anti-terror police (2011)

11   Shaffer (Ludwig von Mises Institute 2009) Boundaries of Order: Private Property As a Social System 47%

learning.The education systems we have cannot be flexible to accommodate the needs of children who learn differently, regardless of their ability. At the extreme end, when we label a child as autistic, or having ADHD, or Asperger's we describe them as having a 'disorder'. Not only are they different, but they are implicitly 'ill-equipped to be educated'; somehow broken. Instead of celebrating the opportunity in this Difference (for example, the increased skills in perception, attention or memory[12] that are sometimes seen in autistic children), the system fails them because it apologises on their behalf, and encourages their parents to believe that it is 'no-one's' fault if their child does not do well. In fact, there is huge opportunity in the difference. The label these children receive negates them, it justifies the system failing them, and says that it is okay for them to not achieve traditional academic success, rather than saying that it is essential that their skills are fostered in a different way.

What we see is that instead of recognising difference as a natural, precious opportunity, our education systems and governments have precious few mechanisms by which to celebrate and take advantage of it. Either they suppress individualism, and integrate it into the norm or, like the case of children with mental 'disorders' they are labeled as deficient, put on a shelf and forgotten about. The only difference between a plant and a weed in our garden is that we don't want the weed to be there. By creating

12   http://goo.gl/5G9duk - The Royal Society: Perception and apperception in autism: rejecting the inverse assumption (2009)

categories of 'disorders' and applying them to our children, we encourage them to underperform when we should be challenging them to help us think differently. When we ask citizens to report deviant thought to the police we encourage fear and mistrust, instead of a forum where ideas can be discussed and understood. we generate a collective subconscious belief that Difference is danger, rather than vitality. And within this system, the three things a country needs to exist - a geographical space with borders, a system of law, and economic well-being - also subconsciously contribute to this conformity. A boundary requires people to be kept within a uniform space, legislation requires people to conform to a uniform set of rules and, perhaps most importantly, economic growth requires the dedication of a nation's people to a common economic goal. Because we can't easily live somewhere else, and we risk punishment by breaking the law, the easy option is conforming to the third; making money in a uniform way rather than finding fulfillment in something unique.

NewSpeak

As we know, there are known knowns; there are things we know we know. We also know there are known unknowns; that is to say we know there are some things we do not know. But there are also unknown unknowns -- the ones we don't know we don't know. And if one looks throughout the history of our country and other free countries, it is the latter category that tend to be the difficult ones. - Donald Rumsfeld, 2002

This quote from Donald Rumsfeld is a kind of strange universal poetry. At the time he was defending the US invasion of Iraq, despite limited evidence of Weapons of Mass Destruction in the country. But Rumsfeld's words of wisdom bear remembering, because they remind us that it is often 'the things we don't know we don't know' that are the most dangerous. There are other means than just law enforcement and violent suppression, by which our thoughts and beliefs are subverted. There is rhetoric and there is propaganda - bending of the truth.

George Orwell's 1984 is set in a world of endless propaganda, engineered poverty and a permanent culture of fear and surveillance, but a far more subversive and fundamental tactic is being deployed by the fascist government; the English language is being slowly reduced in size. Words are how we think, and with a strategic and incremental reduction in the volume of words comes a destruction of thought itself. Nuance, and the capacity for creative, disruptive ideas is being systematically obliterated in 1984 in pursuit of a purely functional language. The idea is that if people are incapable of articulating dissent, then there can be no objection to the party line. Phrases such as "War is Peace. Freedom is Slavery. Ignorance is Strength." show how the government doctrine is literally changing the meaning of words so that the state's belief system is the only possible one.

Does this happen in real life? You bet. And it doesn't just happen within regimes that most people would consider 'oppressive' (well, depending on your perspective on Bush-era, post 9/11 America). The 'War on Terror' was renamed the 'Global Struggle Against Extremism', which sounds innocuous enough, until you consider what 'extremism' actually is.

In and of itself extremism is not an illegal thing; not even necessarily one that is destructive. Crocodile hunter Steve Irwin, Miley Cyrus, even Jesus Christ himself can easily be called 'Extremists' for their lifestyles and beliefs. But we wouldn't label them evil, or criminals, for practicing them (well, apart from maybe Miley).

Maybe the usage wasn't meant in this way, and 'Global Struggle Against Extremism' was supposed to refer to terrorists exclusively. It is true, after all, that this phrase was eventually recast as the 'Global Struggle Against Violent Extremism'. The initial rebranding, though, demonstrates how overzealously the government attempted to co-opt the word. The Bush administration not only co-opted it, in fact, but in many ways succeeded in having us buy into the belief that being 'extreme' is wrong regardless of its context. Extreme views were dangerous; the norm was safe. Eventually, as evidenced by the rise in verbal and physical abuse against Muslim Americans during this period, the 'different' also became the 'extreme'. Being 'different' became being wrong by extension.

One chronic problem with relying on a centralised government body to define how a large group of people should think is that over time our own ability to think for ourselves is eroded. Take a look at the pictures on the following pages:

WARNING

DO NOT TIP OR ROCK
THIS VENDING MACHINE

TIPPING OR ROCKING MAY
CAUSE SERIOUS INJURY
OR DEATH   NBS130

ANTI-THEFT DEVICE PREVENTS
OBTAINING FREE PRODUCT

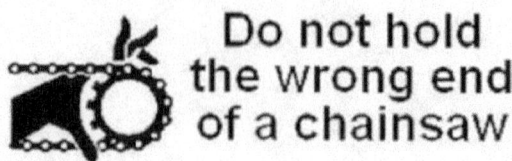

Being spoon-fed these warnings, and having the minutiae of our lives mandated to us eventually diminishes our willingness and ability to make decisions. It infantilises us, and legitimises the kinds of bizarre lawsuits that allow a woman to win $2.7m in damages because no-one told her the coffee she bought would be hot[13]. As more and more of our life is controlled and regulated, we become worse and worse at thinking for ourselves. E.E. Cummings reminds us:

To be nobody but yourself in a world doing its best to make you everybody else means to fight the hardest battle any human can ever fight and never stop fighting.[14]

There are some forward-thinking cities that recognise this, and who have applied the idea of giving people more responsibility over the actions in order to reduce things like traffic accidents. In the Dutch town of Drachten, for example, the city removed traffic lights[15] from the town centre, and because its citizens now had to pay more attention to what they are doing, it saw an eightfold decrease in the number of accidents. Being allowed to think for ourselves, and to think differently, provides us with a safety net for the kind of catastrophic failures that can happen when a government gets it wrong.

---

13   http://goo.gl/eU2v9A - Wikipedia: Liebeck v. McDonald's Restaurants (1994)
14   E.E. Cummings
15   http://goo.gl/yzveK7 - Wikipedia: Drachten (2007)

Money

Jostled by an education system that is trying to turn you into a lawyer, or a software engineer, or a management consultant, it becomes harder to work out what you actually find pleasure in, and the layers of social pressure on top of this, which push you to be financially successful, or professional, or tell you you need a degree, anchor us in a narrow set of beliefs about what is valuable. Once we've gone through the education system, and got our first job, we're already scared of giving up the investment - the sunk costs - that we have in our lives. Our scope of what we could do with our lives is narrowed as each year passes. If we were the hot particles in our newborn exploding universe, it would be as though we were channeled in just one direction, rather than being allowed to spread outwards unrestrained and organically. It makes our aspirations trend towards the norm, and in a big city like London or New York the aspirational norm is being in an airless office cubicle doing finance, or consulting, or some other 'professional service'.

Most people reading this book will have grown up in a culture where money is perceived as a necessity, and where it is also desirable. This means that we easily forget that people have been, can be, and are in many cases happy without making loadsa money. Because we are competitive animals, because we measure our success invariably against the success of others, and because we are taught, from an early age and without deep consideration, that money is desirable, people with very little money aspire to have more, and people with more money aspire to make even more than that.

It is the great wrongheaded lifestyle choice, and it is the quintessential psychodrama of the middle-class 45 year old male; the mid-life crisis. Having expended a youth in the pursuit of money, and being anchored by responsibilities such as a spouse, house and children, the worry sinks in that all of your energy has been expended in the pursuit of something with no real value to you, and that it's now too late to truly pursue that real value, whatever it might be. This leads into the big problem, which is that even if you have a solid idea of what you want to achieve, societal pressure often forces you into the pursuit of money, because it is a 'safer bet'. Untold numbers of young people from wealthy backgrounds with a passion for drawing, or music, or the arts (so many that it is something of a cliché), have been coerced by pushy parents into jobs in law, or finance, or consultancy, even though they have the privilege of a financial safety net that would help them pursue their passion. More insidiously, young people with an aptitude for and enjoyment of something like construction, or sports, or maybe an interest in animals and farming, have been encouraged to disregard such interests in the pursuit of jobs with more of a social cache, and more associated money (like becoming a doctor or an accountant).

This is not to say that people shouldn't make money. Some people are phenomenally good at making money, and some people very much enjoy the social status and accoutrements that come with being wealthy - for some people it may very well be their best shot at happiness. Money is often just a side-effect, though, and what drives some of the wealthiest people in the world is not primarily the acquisition of money and material possessions. Warren Buffett, one of the most successful investors in history, is famously frugal, driving an old sedan and still living in the same house in Omaha that he bought for $31,500 in 1958. Money is often not the end goal for incredibly driven and successful investors and entrepreneurs, and a passion solely for making money is not always the best temperament for acquiring it.

Making money can be difficult, and making a lot of money in a predictable way (i.e. working as a lawyer) takes a long time. People aspiring to the lifestyles of the super-rich and famous begin to foster desires for their own wealth and social status which are incredibly unlikely. Not everyone can win the lottery, and although in the 21st century everyone can be famous for 15 minutes, the luster is unlikely to last.

It is partly because our core nature is to shy away from the grey, office cubicled, clearly laid out paths that are set out for us that we pursue 'fame'. It is because the traditional path to security is so depressing and rigid that young people in dire straits are tempted by high-risk, high pay-off pursuits (like drug-dealing). This is also why we aspire to get-rich-quick but extremely low-probability options, like becoming a professional footballer or winning Pop Idol. Because our televisions, Buzzfeed articles and endless lifestyle magazines are filled with celebrities and their ludicrous, airbrushed lifestyles, we feel that it really can't be that unlikely that we could make it big. The gas stations and restaurants of LA - endlessly staffed by wannabe actors - tell a different story,

Industries and media empires have sprung up to service these misplaced desires (The X Factor, Britain's Next Top Model etc.). When you combine the impossibility of accruing this much wealth & fame through a 'day-job', the growing desire to become rich and famous quickly, as well as the high unlikelihood that it will actually happen, you create a vicious cycle where people have not only unrealistic expectations, but also expectations warped and narrowed by society's belief that it is necessary to be financially wealthy and famous. Added to this, fashions and tastes within the media change very quickly, and the turnover for the next pop band or celebrity TV show is becoming quicker and quicker; you're likely to get dumped just as soon as you think you've made it.

Independence

So what should we be trying to do with our lives, other than just questioning authority?
Living the American Dream in the 21st century is increasingly difficult. The payoff for a lifetime of hard work no longer matches our aspirations, and the freedom and independence we have is coloured from an early age by the desire to acquire wealth. We pursue the money, before we work out what we should actually do with it to make us happy.

The sentiment of the US declaration of independence is noble. It's hard to argue with a 'right' to life, liberty and the pursuit of happiness, and it's hard to argue against the idea that people should achieve success through their merits rather than cronyism; that the state should exist to safeguard our independence, rather than to intervene with a vested interest. The problem, just like we see in England & France, Japan, India and increasingly China is that wealth - rather than what your wealth helps you to achieve - is success in and of itself.

The ideal of 'prosperity' in both the Declaration of Independence and the American Dream, is distorted, and too narrowly portrayed as the acquisition of money. We get stuck at prosperity, and never quite make it to happiness. The realisation that there are non-financial ways to achieve happiness invariably comes too late, just as we're starting to have faith in and realise our own independent perspective. Just as our universe hurtles headlong outwards, dispersing energy until it reaches a cold end-state of thermal equilibrium, our lives also have a limited lifespan. It's essential that we use the energy and passion of our youth in discovering and pursuing our unique goals, and challenging a status quo telling us what we want before we know it. Finding individual passions adds fuel to the fire, and keeps us burning longer.

The only places where government is mentioned in the Declaration of Independence is in enshrining and protecting the rights to "life, liberty and the pursuit of happiness":

To secure these rights, Governments are instituted among Men, deriving their just powers from the consent of the governed, --That whenever any Form of Government becomes destructive of these ends, it is the Right of the People to alter or to abolish it, and to institute new Government, laying its foundation on such principles and organizing its powers in such form, as to them shall seem most likely to effect their Safety and Happiness.

By anyone's measure, governments have overreached this today. Many countries forbid the free exchange of goods and people between countries, wage aggressive and colonialist international wars, regulate and tax private businesses, assassinate the leaders of other states, suppress free speech and undermine the foundations of other governments. It's not a simple matter, though - many officials would tell you that these policies were enacted precisely to protect life, liberty and happiness; that they are the lesser of two evils, and enacted to protect against international aggression, or financial meltdown.

We have to ask in a globalised 21st century whether such a pared down, purist form of government as is outlined in the declaration would be enough to maintain a stable society today. At the moment we sacrifice some freedom of thought, speech and mobility, but we rely on our government to legislate and to maintain peace. As we have seen, Difference is a low priority in our current social contracts. A more decentralised power structure and decision-making process gives us each more freedom, and less authoritarian overhead, but it jeopardises traditional notions of stability and order.

Our individual actions can be harmful to others, and we rely on established conventions of law and order to keep the peace. Without law enforcement it would be much easier for someone to burgle your house and evade punishment, but the counterweight is the chance that you would chase down the burglar and enact your own brand of vigilante justice. We like having established rules and enforcement because it avoids the kind of eye for eye, tooth for tooth vendettas that escalated from these conflicts in pre-feudal times.

There are also some freedoms that we give up willingly. It's in no-one's interests for us to have the 'freedom' to carry around live explosives in built up areas, and in most countries (sorry America) we think it's crazy to let anyone carry around guns in the street without a licence or some training. Some freedoms are so detrimental to the well-being of others that we give them up voluntarily. And that's where the 'praise of Difference' and nonconformism and individuality becomes troublesome. Life is not as black and white as law, and the negative effects of things we do are often bound up with the positive ones. Imagine someday soon a chemist at Pantene invents a cream that uses nanobots to clean your hair and cut it to any style you want. It sounds amazing, and it would save us hundreds of dollars a year. But it would put hairdressers out of business on an international scale. Indirectly it could cripple the styling industry, and shutter cosmetics companies who have relied on a need for shampoo, conditioner, hairspray and moisturising cream, and add tens of billions of dollars to the economy every year. Is Pantene's new cream good for for society?

What if I told you I had invented a machine that would

reduce your commute time by 90%, and let everyone travel across the whole country cheaply and quickly; the only catch being that in order for everyone to use it we would have to sacrifice 40,000 people a year in each country. Would you allow it?

This machine is the motor car. It brought huge advances in industry, freedom and exploration, but it has also cost the lives of millions in road-traffic accidents. Does the indirect impact of our actions on others mean we should ban the man with the nanobot cream from selling it? Does it mean we should have stopped Henry Ford from building his cars? Good things and bad things are rarely isolated from one another in society, and the long-term effects are hard to predict.

As well as social change brought about by improved technology and greater automation of work, individualism and unconventional thought is also responsible for the most disruptive political forces in our history. Non-conformists like Marx, Lenin, Hitler, Mao, Che Guevara, have all left indelible marks on world history, and brought about social advance mixed with great human misery. Almost all of them were persecuted for their views by authority (Lenin and Marx lived in exile, Hitler was imprisoned, Mao's initial labour struggles against the government were suppressed etc.), all of them brought some benefits to some people in their societies (the lifting of hundreds of millions from poverty in China, increase of land and prosperity for the native Germans not persecuted by the NAZI party in Germany, freedom from autocratic rule in Russia), and yet the disruption came at a huge human cost. Tens of millions died during famines in China, millions of Jews were killed under Hitler's rule, and millions were killed or starved to death during the civil war and subsequent Soviet rule.

These are extreme cases, but illustrate that extreme ideas and extreme individuals are disruptive, and that this disruption almost never brings just benefits or just harm to a society. The downsides of absolute conformism, though, are even greater. Like Huxley's Brave New World, throttling human creativity and independent thought throttles our reason for being alive in the first place.

If we swung further in the direction of conformism and orthodoxy, we would have a society where a central authority is far more in control of our lives and work, and which intervenes more in the day to day running of things. What are the dangers? More controlling governments place more of an emphasis on nationalism, on one righteous path. The individuals within them are largely encouraged to work towards goals for their countrymen, and not to think about the humanity of foreigners. Conflict is projected outwards, and national problems are directed at international powers to maintain inner solidarity. We saw this in Russia and the USSR during the cold war, and we see it in the xenophobic politics of far-right parties like UKIP in the UK, blaming immigrants for social problems. At the extreme end, we have ideological insularity, and the kind of brittle nationalism crystallised in modern-day North Korea.

This kind of mass 'uniformity of thought' provides the

perfect storm for large-scale conflict. The more decentralised a society, and the more diverse its viewpoints, the less likely it is that people are borne along in a groundswell of nationalism and shallow rhetoric. It becomes more difficult for a state to conscript an army, or to unilaterally declare an enemy.

In a country of tens or hundreds of million people, any issue that can unite everyone has to be very abstract. Most people don't care about corn exports, or the nuances of agricultural policy. Some might care about child labour, but not about arranged marriages. People care about such different things, that to unite them we have to use general principles.

The issues that are used to unite people in big countries are generalised almost to the point of unmeaning. How can you disagree that we should stop evil-doers, rogue states or broken societies? Unfortunately these terms gloss over the details of the conflict or problem, and shield people from the often uncomfortable consequences of the situation, often until it is too late. The 'War on Terror' is a good example of this - a crusade against 'evil-doers' with 'WMDs' that found no WMDs at all, and left the US with a huge financial burden, thousands of Americans spending years away from their families, and a destructive power-vacuum in the Middle-East. Large groups of people willingly mobilise against others for abstract reasons, and create large-scale violence and warfare that would never happen if the issues could be explained less generally, to smaller groups of people with different priorities.

'Difference of opinion' is not a bad thing. Better to have smaller groups of people arguing than large groups of people united in blowing each other up. Difference of opinion and diversity of backgrounds also make up much of the pleasure and color that we get from social interaction. One of the greatest pleasures of living in a multicultural society comes from the diversity of appearances, viewpoints, backgrounds and experiences that people have, and learning from them. Talking about different countries and practices, trying foreign food, learning a new language; all these things help us work out what we like and what we want. Being Different is not bad; it allows us to learn faster and experience more than we would if people were the same. The celebration and exploration of difference has given us our greatest art, music, invention, industry and philosophical thinking - the influence of Asia on 19th century European art was profound; cultural melting pots like the Harlem Renaissance provided new styles of music and cultural critiques.

Inequality and Difference

'Inequality' is typically described as a material problem. It is framed as wealth inequality. Like abstract nationalist messages of good and evil, this is a dangerously narrow and general view of inequality. It's used by the media because it is easy to comprehend, and by the government because it is a simple concept to which solutions can be proposed; it allows the easy pointing of fingers. What it misses are the nuances mentioned above, and how they shape a world with more depth of inequality than just income; many that can't be 'solved' or 'balanced'. It reduces debate in public around individual happiness and fulfillment to a question of money; the idea that if we just have more money we'll 'solve' societal problems.

We rarely hear from politicians or the mass media about the value of a personally fulfilling life, and that our individual needs will be different from those of the people we know. Instead, we hear about the importance of a financially secure career, a good school and university education, and the importance of narrowing the income gap.

That's not to say that wealth inequality does not cause turmoil in society. It does, especially when wealth inequality is divided along lines of gender or race. The prevailing public debate does little to solve the problem, though, and rarely engages citizens in fruitful searches for a solution that don't just involve providing people with the opportunity for more wealth. It would be pretty dangerous for a country to start telling people not to worry about making money and to just try and be happy.

Using whether you have less, more, or the same amount of money as someone else is an unhelpful benchmark for happiness, and it is one perpetuated by governments, as well as people who want you to buy things, for obvious reasons. Studies on measuring 'happiness' are hard to validate, given how abstract happiness is, and how different happiness is for each of us, but they do tend to show a sharp plateau just above the level at which we have enough money to pay for the things we need, and some money to pay for things we want. Unfortunately, the narrow view of equality and happiness as a function of financial gain is perpetuated. It narrows how we think about our own satisfaction in life, encourages the pursuit of materialistic, moneymaking careers, and leads us away from radical thought, and action which would upset the existing financial system.[16]

Difference means smaller and more diverse. Difference means difference of opinion, but it doesn't mean conflict. Acknowledging that Different does not mean Bad stops the towering propaganda machines that lead countries to war, and helps us understand that our needs are more complex than the need of a country or business to make money. Instead of brittle belief systems that requires one truth and one way of doing things - the kind of brutal systems that have created revolution in Egypt and Syria - Difference creates less fragile networks of understanding, where we can see that other people's needs are different from our own, and not necessarily wrong. Maybe it's ok for a man to love another man even if most men like women. Maybe it's ok for some people to believe in a higher power if it makes them happy, or to not worship a God if they don't want to.

---

16   "Creativity necessitates change, and change is a most uneven process. By contrast, the doctrine of equality is premised on a commitment to inflexibility and nonvariation (and with it, the suppression of individual liberty), requiring the maintenance of equilibrium conditions that further the entropic decline of a society. This is why, contrary to our accustomed thinking, political systems based on egalitarian sentiments (eg. state socialism, welfarism, social leveling) are inherently conservative in nature." Shaffer (Ludwig von Mises Institute 2009) Boundaries of Order: Private Property As a Social System 65%

Radically different ideas create risk, because radical change affects us in both good and bad ways. But a world of conformism is a stagnant world where our uniqueness is effaced, and where one person at the top can make sweeping decisions which affect millions of people. In a world of Difference it's harder to do that. Smaller groups of people who have come to an understanding stand a far lower chance of causing big disasters, and are far more likely to work out what makes them, as individuals, happy.

Do not conform.

Where you are and who you are

Define yourself along personal lines that are meaningful for you. You are not who you have been told you are.

Spanning the border between North and South Korea are two small, blue buildings. One building has a room, half of which is in North Korea, and half in South Korea. South Korean soldiers on one side look uneasily at their North Korean counterparts on the other, and between them both is a table, half in North Korea, half in South Korea. It is around this table that negotiations between the two countries - now divided by a vast cultural gulf, as well as a geographical one - used to be held.

Borders mark a line of territory, but they also mark a line of culture and identity, often in the most peculiar ways. During the partition of the Ottoman Empire at the end of the first World War, Winston Churchill allegedly claimed that he outlined the border of modern-day Jordan "with the stroke of a pen one Sunday afternoon in Cairo." The oddly geometric outline of the Jordanian borders gave rise to speculation that Churchill had hiccupped while drawing this portion, creating the sharp point of Saudi territory wedged deep into Jordan. This point is informally known as "Winston's Hiccup".[17] As arbitrary as they may be, the cultural differences across border lines are etched deeply into our psyches as human beings. They are a core part of our identity, and often the part that we are least willing to surrender. Starting with national borders, this chapter explores the different cultural influences that shape our identity as we grow, so that we can understand who we've been told we are, and who we want to be. It explores the influences on our sense of self, and the restrictions on who we can be within the systems of which we are a part.

"I'm from British Gas"

If you got into conversation with someone in the streets of a foreign country, or in the back of a cab, they would notice your accent. Instead of asking about your family, or job, or interests they would probably begin with the tried-and-true conversation starter: "Where are you from?" In getting to know someone, and understanding who they are, our first instinct is to ask them about the one thing in their life over which they had the least control.

You would probably answer, "I'm English," or, "I'm from Spain," or "I was born in Taiwan, and brought up in America". You wouldn't think of saying, "I'm from British Gas," or "I'm from the pharmaceutical industry", and if you

---

17   Paraphrased from 'Conclusion: Borders in a changing Global Context' in Diener & Hagen (Rowman & Littlefield 2010) Borderlines and Borderlands: Political Oddities at the Edge of the Nation-State Pg. 189

said, "I'm from the Communist party," or, "I'm from the Wallace family", you probably wouldn't get very far in the conversation. The most fundamental unit of our being - our origin - is bound up with our national identity. You wouldn't say, "I'm from inside my mum", even though it's pretty much the most precise answer you could give.

For almost all of us national identity underpins our upbringing; it is how we see ourselves compared to the rest of the world. Our national identity has benefits because it gives us a network of sympathisers, and people who identify with us. In a material sense it gives us our status as a citizen, and in some countries access to welfare services like healthcare. Our passport is what allows us to be accepted into foreign countries - we require a nation in order to go to a new one.

Perhaps most importantly, every country uses the sense of national identity and belonging to unify its people under a shared feeling of what is right. Across the world, the Stars and Stripes and 'The American dream' are two of the most potent symbols in Western culture, let alone American politics. The British Bulldog and the George Cross are iconic symbols of the United Kingdom. Rule Britannia is the song of the British Navy. The teams for all of our global sporting competitions (football, tennis, the olympics) are separated across national boundaries, and major sporting events are an occasion for national pride and solidarity. In many countries it is a crime to destroy or desecrate the national flag.

For every human being alive, their nationality was an

accident of birth; they did not choose it. And yet nationality is how our government makes a distinction between citizens and foreigners, how our political parties justify on a moral level who should receive help, and childcare, and a home, and who should not.

As a child the UK made sense - it was surrounded by water on all sides, so it was clear where it ended, and why. The countries in Europe run straight into one other, but in my child mind there were picket fences in straight or wandering lines down every inch of the divide. I never wondered who put the fences there, and I think I assumed that as each of the countries had grown from some singular middle-point and met another, they had stopped. As I grew up I learned about how countries went to war, and won bits of land off one another in battles, but words like 'raped and pillaged' were not used until later on. Between the Romans, the Saxons, the Vikings and the Normans it seemed that England had at some point been run by everyone else in Europe. As a young person I remember being confused that it seemed as though the only thing deciding where the borders were were a succession of unpleasant and bloody disputes. With the image of the picket fences in my mind, I asked my parents how they had really been decided.

As an adult some of that naivety is gone, but we still don't question that countries need physical, geographical boundaries. States have had to protect their borders from pirates, invading armies and illegal immigrants for so long that the lines on the map feel as real as the flag that flies at the top of the pole. In reality, national boundaries -

geographical ones - are defined first in the minds of conquerors who take the land, then by the fences they build, and then in the minds of those who grow up within them. These new borders become the basis of their identity. They have been 'agreed' as a compromise between groups to maintain peace - drawn up by officials and politicians on maps; or settled upon due to some arbitrary divider - a river, or a mountain, or a sea. Up until recently I was still naive - I believed that in the 21st century the age of violent conquest had been surpassed by one of globalised soft power. Then Russia invaded the Ukraine, and I was forced to think again.

It's hard to deny that a country needs a border. Without a physical area where laws are valid and can be enforced, it becomes difficult to maintain order. Enforcing these laws builds a shared identity, and contributes to the definition of citizens, the creation of trade agreements, and the protection of land or valuable natural resources. But in the 21st century borders are becoming difficult to maintain. The Internet means we can buy things from merchants on the other side of the world, and cyber-crime means that someone can attack a country's infrastructure without ever setting foot in it.

And yet, for all that the world feels more 'global', crossing national borders is still rigidly binary. We see the intimidating border police and wait, bored and puffy-eyed from the flight, in a debilitating line, before stepping up to the rubicon of the customs and immigration desk. We are at the mercy of the bureaucrat in the box as to whether we are in or out.

Blurred boundaries

As arbitrary as the borders were when they were drawn up, crossing that customs line transports us 'somewhere else', whether it's to our holiday - and thoughts of sun, sand and sea - or whether it's to somewhere alien, where we find local customs strange and distasteful. It's even stranger when you think that by the time you 'cross the border' into a new country, your plane or train or boat has already landed in another country.

Stranger still is when you yourself in 'another country' without even realising it.

The Bedouin are a nomadic people originating in Saudi Arabia over 1000 years ago. For centuries, they have been traveling across national borders without belonging to any particular nationality. In the late 19th century, the Ottoman Empire saw their continual 'violation' of national borders as a threat to the cohesion of their state. To the Bedouin - if you'll forgive the pin - the notion of 'state borders' was a foreign concept. For a time, they resisted a settled lifestyle, and when the government attempted to settle them by providing concrete houses and fixed abodes, they used the buildings as shelter for their animals. Many Bedouin are now undergoing 'forced settlement'. Although their nomadic tradition pre-dates the countries through which they travel, their identity must now conform to these new boundaries. They are one example of a diverse body of nomadic peoples who belong to no state, and they are a sadly marginalised example of a powerful culture and identity that can exist without the shadow-lines of national boundary. There are also people who, through accident of birth, become citizens of a certain nation, but identify with another that has no clearly defined geographical border.

The Kurds are a community with a shared identity. Kurdistan has a culture, a history, even a flag. What they do not have, is a 'land' in the traditional sense. Like the Jewish communities who tried to found a homeland before the creation of modern-day Israel, they are a community divided between several nations. After the fall of the Ottoman Empire (seriously Ottomans?!) Kurdish land was divided up and allocated to surrounding countries and other empires. Kurdistan is usually referred to as a 'geo-cultural region' spread across eastern Turkey, northern Iraq, northwestern Iran and northern Syria; a region bounded only by the people within it who self-identify as Kurds. The area that falls within Iraq - Iraqi Kurdistan - has autonomy from the Iraqi government, and Syrian Kurds recently took advantage of the civil war to attempt to carve out a Kurdish territory from Syrian rule. Although Kurdistan's boundaries are undetermined, the region has a very real geopolitical existence. The debate is not whether the region exists, but rather its extent, its unity, and its independence. Communities united by factors other than geographical borders or proximity can grow and thrive today; they exist already, and threaten the relevance of nation states. The Bedouin and the Kurds are outliers in our world, but they demonstrate the possibility of difference; that identity can exist without nationality.

Because of the way in which nations enforce borders we

use words like 'immigration', 'entry' and 'exit', rather than 'migration' or 'movement'. We grow up within a nation, which just by existing defines what is outside its walls as 'other'. Over time, that 'other' becomes what is foreign to us. As well as defining what is outside, it also helps us define what is inside, what it is that makes us in our country unique.

Some of this, you could argue, is just human nature. You need to be cool enough to sit with the cool kids at lunch, you need to be smart enough to get into the good college - building communities of 'people like us' and excluding those who are different is what makes societies cohesive and successful. Today, though, we often have much more in common with foreign people than with our fellow citizens. Big international cities like London, or San Francisco, or Shanghai, or Tokyo, have far more in common with one another than with other cities in their country. They are densely networked, more urban, they share similar industries like Tech and Finance, and their inhabitants share a similar average income. In some cases it's more easy to get from one to another, than to get somewhere else within the country. Flying intercontinental from New York to London takes under 6 hours, but getting from New York to Booneville, Mississippi (less than one third the distance) would take you almost twice as long. Likewise, smaller and more remote cities increasingly have more in common with their international cousins than with the big cities within the border.

The Californian Chemistry professor likely to identify more with his neighbour - who is a professional footballer - or with his friend from Hamburg who teaches Biology at the university there? Is a day labourer working on construction in Dubai likely to have more in common with a resident oil sheikh, or with a builder in neighbouring Saudi Arabia? For better or worse, similarities in terms of the factors that make up our identity - our upbringing, friends, education and jobs - increasingly supersede geographical boundaries.

Who is foreign?

Giving up our sense of 'national identity' feels unnatural and unintuitive. By the time we're adults it's realistically impossible, as notions of home and 'foreignness' have been reinforced in our lives since we were children. Additionally, by the time we're adults we probably do exhibit many of the stereotypes of our countrymen, whether it's English politeness, German punctuality or vigorous mediterranean gesticulating. The sense of belonging we get from having a 'home country' and shared, recognisable characteristics contributes powerfully to our self-confidence, and is easy fodder for small-talk and jokes in unfamiliar places. Trying to consciously discard characteristics we recognise in ourselves, and in which we find happiness, doesn't really make sense. What we should be conscious of, though, is how our sense of self and belonging affects how we understand others. Given our increasingly globally networked world, it's likely that there are far more people outside our country than within it who share our interests, desires and passions. People whose morals and aspirations are closer to our own are likely to want a society more like the one we want, regardless of whether they were born next door, live in the Congo, or swam across an ocean to enter our country 'illegally'. Under the banner of protecting jobs for citizens and saving public money, governments deny immigrants employment, education and services like healthcare. We are told implicitly that foreign people are a threat. But there is overwhelming statistical evidence that immigrants - illegal or otherwise - provide disproportionately large benefits to countries they move to - Rationalwiki has some good stats on the US here[18]. In fact in the US, the sheer volume of illegal immigrants in the US (some 11 million[19] in 2013 according to Pew) mean that the country's economy would at present not be able function without them.

When we start to think about 'who we are' it might be better to think about who we want to be, rather than where we've come from - from this moment we have much more control over the former than the latter. If we do that, we open ourselves up to personal growth, instead of entrenching existing beliefs within the limited perspective we were born into. People with different backgrounds and life experiences teach us things about ourselves or the world that we can't know otherwise, and the more people we engage with, the more likely we are to find people who share our individual passions and can ignite new ones, rather than reinforcing existing dogma and preconceptions.

---

18   http://goo.gl/HSjYxL - Rationalwiki: Myths and facts about immigration to the United States

19   http://goo.gl/9pY4PQ - New York Times: Number of Illegal Immigrants in U.S. May Be on Rise Again, Estimates Say (2013)

We can complain until the end of time about how unfair it is that states make the decision on whether or not we get to enter a country. What is important is that we question whether the things we were taught hold true - that immigration is dangerous, that geographical borders are in our own interests. Today our homeland is the beginning of our identity, but it shouldn't be the border of our identity.

Blondes have more fun

Your nation is not the be-all and the end-all of your identity. It is also not the only contributing factor. Genetic factors like our skin or hair colour influence the way that we are treated by society; our family and relationship with our parents shapes our early education and world-view; our friends shape our sense of self-worth and peer relations; the town we grow up in gives us our first opportunity to place ourselves in a wider world; the news media we consume influences our sense of right and wrong; our education we receive and the television we watch shape our opinions and understanding of that world; the list goes on and on and on. Who we are and who we think we are is a kaleidoscope of our genes and our upbringing and how we interact with the big wide world.

At each stage of our life and growth the information we receive becomes less concrete, and harder to judge objectively. As an example, we are acutely aware of our own body - the sensations we feel, what we look like in the mirror, what we enjoy eating, who we find attractive and what side of the bed we like to sleep on. Although they're not infallible, our own senses and thoughts are the most 'knowable'.

In parents we have the opinions of two people who are similar to us genetically, but who are more worldly and (usually) have our best interests at heart. They're the first guides we have through the world. At school our peer group will typically share a similar upbringing and some social values, and differ on others. The opinions we receive from them - that this band is good, that this type of shirt is ugly, that we should bully the fat kid - are a result of an even broader set of upbringings and information. They're still somewhat 'democratic' in that - aside from the mass media - they are the amalgamated opinions of a large body of people. However, as the circle (or system) gets bigger, the opinions we are pressured by our peers to conform to (taste in clothes, music etc.) become more generalised. We become exposed to trends and fashions that are sweeping the country, rather than just our schoolyard, or just our household (if you have a really big family!).

In the case of a government, which unites people through broad moral and political consensus, the decision-making group is extremely small compared to the reach and power that it has. A global network of billions of people contribute to online discussions about music and fashion. The Internet can support millions of different opinions, and although sites like Reddit exist to aggregate majority consensus, Difference thrives.

The reason that this is important, and the way in which it affects our sense of personal identity - our notion of who we are - is that today's governments are not like Reddit. They are not decentralised enough to cater to millions of specific needs, and they have a limited opportunity to communicate with their people. When they do, they are typically communicating with a whole country. Specific messages like "we have categorised this 3 kilometre section of woodland in Southampton as a protected site for the badger population" would be irrelevant to many. With limited airtime and (at least in most of what we call democracies) a need to be re-elected governments need to be seen to be taking action of which people approve, and to have that approval be as broad as possible.

Summed up beautifully by SMBC[20], we end up with a watered-down "More Betterness, Less Worseness". It's hard to eliminate political rhetoric, but focusing our notion of identity away from the abstract mass messages of governments gets us closer to understanding who we are, rather than what a ruling body thinks we want them to be supporting. Basing our identities around a centralised, national voice becomes particularly problem is in situations involving conflict and war. From both sides of the two world wars, propaganda demonises the other side with generalisations (Soviets become fat, stupid alcoholics, NAZI troops are shown bayoneting babies). Because war requires the mobilisation of large groups of people against large groups of people who have never met one another, the way in which the enemy is described tends towards the same abstraction. 'They' are represented in as homogenous and evil a way as is realistically possible, so

---

20   http://goo.gl/ShUuxt - SMBC: Consistency

that 'we' can believe we are right, and justify violence as a means to an end.

The ability to differentiate, and to identify difference and complexity, is an integral part of understanding. Identity is formed just as much by understanding what you are not as what you are (i.e. I am not as wealthy as that person, I am more attractive than him, I am kinder than her). But when that 'difference' is applied in an abstract and blanket way to a large group of people, for example "America is a land of fat, greedy people, and being greedy is evil", the capacity for misunderstanding is broad, and people can quite easily end up acting on beliefs that are either widely inaccurate or wrong. Violence, when a large group of people are convinced of their blanket righteousness, is far more destructive. Nationalism can be used for positive means, like raising money for the victims of natural disasters, or in solidarity and support in the face of terrorist attacks, like the 9/11 bombing of the World Trade Center. But charitable giving also transcends national boundaries. Within 7 days of the 2010 Haiti earthquake, $275m had been raised across the world. A huge number of people who had no connection with the disaster identified with the humanitarian struggle, and offered support.

An Englishman's home is his castle

So goes the adage in the land of drizzle and warm beer. Even outside of the UK, though, house and home are a core part of who we are. For the lucky amongst us, home is a symbol of refuge and family. It's where we return during the holidays to eat and drink and celebrate with our loved ones - it's an even deeper, more emotional part of who we are than the country we're from, or the city we grew up in. It's where our parents raised us, where we fought with our siblings and it's at the heart of our identity. Our homes and land - if we're lucky enough to have bought them - are the closest we come to owning something permanent, and we return to our parents' homes with an ever more powerful nostalgia as we grow up.

Home feels permanent and unshakeable, but in reality we have very little authority over the land we 'own'. The English - colonised first by the Romans, then the Saxons, then the Vikings and finally the Normans - knew this acutely; ownership was only worth as much as your ability to defend the land from someone else. 800 years after the Norman invasion, Jim Saleet of Lakewood, Ohio, was about to discover the same.

Jim was a retired pharmaceutical worker, and one day in 2009 he and his wife Joanne, were told by Lakewood City that they had to move out of their home, which they owned and had bought. Jim's had worked 38 years of his life to pay off the mortgage and 'own' the land and the home, but was told abruptly that the building would soon be demolished so that new, more expensive condominiums could be built by the city council. The Saleets were told they would be offered 'fair market value' for their land - a calculation that wouldn't take into account the cost of moving, wouldn't reimburse them for any business losses if they had a home business, and which paid no mind to the 38 years of history they had built there. And when we say 'offered' it's a little bit of a misnomer; the Saleets had no choice about whether to move out or not.

At the time CBS news covered this case[21] as just one of many abuses of what is known legally and obscurely as "eminent domain" - a government's ability to seize property 'for the public good'. Lakewood's mayor at the time defended the action, saying that Lakewood's aging tax base had been shrinking, and that the city simply needed more money. In violating their home the mayor was not only demolishing a building, but bulldozing family memories and the legacy of the family's whole working life - almost 4 decades that had gone into creating what the Saleets had. "I thought I bought this place." Jim says at the end of the article, "But I guess I just leased it, until the city wants it." As much as you believe, that you 'own' your house and the land on which it stands, this is rarely the case. At best we are leaseholders with poor terms.

Many countries have similar policies on forcibly 'purchasing' land from landowners (in the UK it is the slightly more straightforward 1994 Compulsory Purchase of Land Act). The grounds (if you'll forgive the pun) on which the land may be seized vary from country to country, but are generally couched in vague legal terminology that is open to interpretation, and abuse.

Like the US, in the UK citizens' property can be seized in areas where the seizure is deemed "for the public benefit". In the past this has included removing houses to build a

---

21   http://goo.gl/B0IAhC - CBS: Eminent Domain: Being Abused? (2003)

public swimming pool, clearing away gardens and allotments to create new motorways, and destroying streets to build a munitions factories to build shells to kill people and win wars. It has in the past been exercised by the local councils of places like Cornwall to threaten people into leasing out their unoccupied houses, and by islands like Alderney to force residents out of areas where the state wanted to build an airport. It is often a tool of last resort, but because of this the existing 'landowners' are given no choice whether to settle for the offer they are given. The payment citizens receive is not a payment at open market rates, and there is no negotiation. It is decided by tribunal, at a price imagined as that agreed 'between a willing seller and a willing purchaser'. In the end, our homes, and the only parts of our identities and histories that are tied to a physical space we own, are sold as though we wanted them gone. That states exercise this power at all shows that civil liberties, and the desires of individuals, are far from sacrosanct.

As well as creating arbitrary borders, and exercising sovereign ownership of the land inside them, governments also maintain strict boundaries from one another, and rigorous border control to stop people entering and leaving as they please. Border control and migration might not seem - on the surface - like attempts to turn you into someone you're not, or restrictions on you becoming who you want to be, but restricting movement through the myriad cities and cultures of the earth restricts our depth of experiences and our exposure to ideas. Before the Internet and global news media, restricting the flow of people restricted the flow of information and ideas, and kept us in the kind of isolation we now lament in North Korea.

Some groups of people, such as those living within the Eurozone of EU members, have more freedom to travel and work within the member states of the continent. If you were a British citizen by birth, you could move to France or Germany, rent an apartment and get a job without much hassle from the government. This isn't common for most parts of the world. If a British person wanted to just visit the US, for example, they would be limited to spending 90 days there, without being allowed to work or look for a job. If you wanted to move there to work you would need to prove you had employment there, and complete an expensive VISA application process. In some countries, like China, it is difficult for citizens to obtain an individual VISA just to leave the country. The passports of US citizens mandate some countries which its citizens are forbidden from entering (Cuba & North Korea). As some parts of Europe (like the UK) become increasingly xenophobic, migration laws are tightening. More diverse cities and counties tend to be less racist or xenophobic, and more open minded. Conversely, restricting immigration exacerbates a spiral into isolationism and xenophobia.

Stopping the flow of people into a country is one thing, but removing a citizen's freedom to leave a country is far more draconian, and a far more deliberate and insidious way to repress people's growth and desires. In a connected 21st century, where information about other countries and lifestyles is available across the borders of most nations, people living in poor or oppressive conditions may want to leave, rather than stay and suffer. Rather than working to improve conditions for its people, and conscious that it needs a workforce to generate revenue, it may seem easier in the short term for a nation to just close its borders and physically stop people from leaving. In the past China has made it very difficult for people to obtain individual VISAs to leave; in Soviet Russia it was similarly difficult. In present day North Korea it's almost impossible; people try to escape by smuggling themselves and their families across the border, or swimming across illegally. Many die.

Borders and Order

There is a commonly held belief in liberal countries that you are free to come and go from your home country unless you have done something wrong. Governments typically use the term 'Reasonable grounds' when they have reason to believe that a citizen they're detaining is involved in illegal business, but can't yet prove it. It's another of those deliberately vague terms like which can be open to abuse, but people generally agree that if someone has been acting illegally within a country, then apprehending them at the border is a reasonable thing to do. Visitors have to be subjected to the laws of the country they are in so that order can be maintained.

That said, the media within a country like the UK or the US often balk when the citizens of that country are subjected to the alien laws of a foreign nation.
In Dubai British citizens have been imprisoned and severely punished for public displays of affection (in one case a couple had sex on a beach in Dubai). In another, a hapless tourist was imprisoned for accidentally bringing

chewing gum into Singapore (this was, at the time, banned). In more surreal circumstances, British 'plane-spotters' - a niche group of hobbyists - have been detained under suspicion of being military spies. In all cases the visitors were breaking the other countries' laws.

The coverage these stories receive is sensationalist, and ignores the foreign country's need to enforce law within its borders. The result is xenophobia; the coverage is designed to make foreign countries seem backward or oppressive, and it engorges national pride at home - the sense that our country knows the 'right' way of doing things. It warps our understanding of foreign cultures and customs, and marginalises our ability to empathise with people who are different. It does, though, sell newspapers.

We can understand the practical reason why countries need to enforce their borders, but what's harder to explain is why they have the right to. At the beginning of this chapter we looked at how national borders are subjective and conceptual - how they were almost invariably formed by a mixture of natural features (seas and mountain ranges) and border disputes. In absolute terms, it is hard to justify why a state has any right to stop you from entering its land. You can see why a society might not want you to use the public services that its people work hard to build and fund, but it's very important in understanding 'national identity' that claiming the land (and keeping you off it) is really only based on the fact that someone else managed to get there first, and has more power than you do to keep you out.

If you're reading this book I'll keep my fingers crossed your society has gone beyond serfdom, and that the kind of situations that were common until the 1800s (where families like the Liechtensteins could literally buy your country and put you to work on the land) can't really happen any more. And I'll keep my toes crossed that you don't think that 'might is right' - that the ability to take land by force is a justification for keeping it. If you thought this, the British Empire would still stretch across the world, and Austria might still be united with Germany. The fact that an army your family led won a war three-hundred years ago is not a good reason for you to run a country.

The consequences of our violent and power-hungry past, though, very much dictate borders today, and they dictate our national identity as well as strongly influencing our personal one. When the taxi driver asks you where you're from and you say "England", that single identifier carries with it Empire, slavery and the colonization of much of the known world. That is the context within which you are choosing to identify yourself, and even though national sovereignty becomes a core part of how we identify ourselves, it's something that governments themselves rarely respect.

In 2008, for example, the German government was frustrated that it was missing out on tax revenue. German foreign intelligence believed that wealthy citizens were avoiding tax by storing it in anonymous bank accounts based in Liechtenstein, but unfortunately these banks were outside of Liechtenstein's control. Germany had its foreign intelligence agents bribe a disgruntled former employee of the trusts division of the Liechtenstein's LGT bank to turn over a stolen computer disc containing roughly 1,400 names of foreign account holders. Armed with this incriminating list, Germany immediately began cracking down on hundreds of its citizens who appeared guilty of tax fraud. The Germans also shared the list with tax authorities in other countries[22], which led to a slew of demands on the individuals who held money with LGT.

At any given time there is a tacit peace between most nations. When it suits them, though, governments are quite happy to send people into another country and break the local laws in order to protect their financial interests. No state treats the borders of another as sacrosanct, and our recent past is full of border violations - Russia's incursion in Ukraine, America's full-scale invasion of Iraq, French intervention in Libya, the UK government's plans drawn up to storm the Ecuadorian Embassy (which is Ecuadorian land), and apprehend Julian Assange. Increasingly, the violations also do not need to be 'physical'; cyberwarfare between China and the US is ongoing and massive in scale, and the Stuxnet attack in Iran still has a lot of unanswered questions. The deniability of cyber-attacks by nation-states is one of their most attractive qualities.

Cronyism between heads of state and heads of business also erodes the morality of our governments. Private businesses have huge lobbying groups, and friends in high

22   Ostergren 'Defining Liechtenstein: Sovereign Borders, Offshore Banking, and National Identity" in Diener & Hagen (Rowman & Littlefield 2010) Borderlines and Borderlands: Political Oddities at the Edge of the Nation-State Pg. 146

places who exert cast influence on legislation. In some cases - as with Silvio Berlusconi or Hank Paulson - heads of state are heads of business - a President can be a media mogul, and an executive at Goldman Sachs can be Secretary of State. These people muddy the waters further and for their own interests. Our nations become vehicles for personal greed, and this reflects on how other people perceive us.

Nations act out of self-interest, to protect their own stability and growth. That's why China hacks America, America spies on Germany and Russia basically gives everyone else the finger. We use our home countries as a proxy for our identity, but having such amoral home countries colours perceptions of us as individuals.

Our home country influences who we are even before we're born. Trade agreements and healthcare influence the kind of pregnancy our mother will have, and culture and beliefs influence how we will be delivered into the world. As we grow up notions of country and nation shape our understanding of the world. The needs of a state (border, laws and economic growth) influence where we can go, what we can do, who we should trust, what we can know and - most importantly - what we value. It becomes a core, inalienable part of our identities, but it should not define us.

State borders are relics forged in violent or colonialist power-struggle. They were not designed in the interests of the happiness of citizens. Even in the most 'democratic' nations our notion of home as discrete from nation (the family house we grow up in, or the land we grew up on) is jeopardised. Land we 'own' can be taken away arbitrarily, and houses bulldozed with impunity.

Prejudice against an ideological or geographical 'other' is an inherent part of our mass media, our education, and what our government tells us. Every day we hear about the danger of 'Rogue states' like Iran, Somali immigrants or Russian aggression. But the people in these countries are not their country, and the closing of borders - whether physically or ideologically - is what creates a concept of 'foreignness'. It delineates an arbitrary distinction, and stops us from properly understanding what other people in the world are like. The fact that America now tacitly collaborates with Iran against Islamic State, and that the immigrants threatening our jobs now come from Poland rather than Somalia, shows how opportunistically these targets are chosen. It suggests that we're safer being skeptical, and will deepen our understanding of the world by defining our identity along shared values with individuals across the world, rather than subscribing to a dogmatic stereotype which teaches us to reject Difference.

States use their borders as much to stop people from leaving as to stop people from entering. For a government the borders are a tool of necessity, used to secure ideological and geographical power, rather than the happiness of citizens. This is summed up in the book Borderlines and Borderlands: Political Oddities at the Edge of the Nation-State, in describing post-soviet Uzbekistan:

For the Uzbekistani government...their border was not

merely the location of Uzbekistan's defense of its territory and security. It was also a moral border, a cartography of knowledge mapping a geopolitical vision of vulnerable post-soviet political space that enabled the Uzbek elite to write its authority over the material and social landscapes of Uzbekistan [23]

We are lucky now to live in a world where the Internet has enabled information and knowledge to cross borders, although China's Great Firewall still holds, and governments across the world are making inroads into blocking content they'd rather you didn't see. Russia[24] recently blocked all of GitHub, Turkey[25] temporarily blocked Youtube, and the UK[26] - prudish as ever - is uncomfortable about the pornography you watch. Added to this, governments recognise the power of social networks in unifying people against authoritarian doctrine, which is why when Syria and Egypt descended into revolution, access to the Internet was one of the first things to be cut. Governments have a vested interest in defining who you are by what you know.

---

23   Megoran 'The Uzbekistan-Kyrgyzstan Boundary: Stalin's Cartography, Post-Society Geography' in Diener & Hagen (Rowman & Littlefield 2010) Borderlines and Borderlands: Political Oddities at the Edge of the Nation-State Pg. 45

24   http://goo.gl/xJvK31 - Techcrunch: Russia Blacklists, Blocks GitHub Over Pages That Refer To Suicide (2014)

25   http://goo.gl/IytH7b - CNN: Turkey blocks YouTube days after Twitter crackdown (2014)

26   http://goo.gl/988oAq - Guardian: David Cameron's internet porn filter is the start of censorship creep (2014)

It's really hard to opt out of living in a country, though, no matter how much they colour who we are - almost all of the world's land is claimed by someone, and there are some very basic things (like law enforcement and healthcare) that we rely on a big system to provide. In fact, that's part of the reason why countries can get away with doing things which are so restrictive, and still continue to have authority; if there was always somewhere else we could go, they might have to try a bit harder to be less oppressive.

So realistically, if we want to follow the spirit of the E.E. Cummings quote and 'be nobody but ourselves in a world doing its best to make us everybody else', what can we actually do? If we want to stay wise to propaganda and dogma, express ourselves in unconventional ways, travel to places that might be forbidden, and speak to people out of our reach, how do we do it? One thing is to challenge dogma - to question what you're told, and to define yourself along personal lines that are meaningful for you.The other might just be to wait a little bit.

End States

The geographical borders of today's nation states are less relevant than they once were. Information on the Internet has a global reach, Cyber-crime means international attacks can take place from the comfort of your desk, and the international subcontracting of work (think FoxConn in China and call-centers in India) has slowed the huge migrations of the 19th and 20th centuries. This has also meant that millions of people work remotely and - in a sense - live internationally. You can live in India but make money for and from an American company.

In the last centuries England has seen significant waves of Indian and Pakistani immigrants, America has had waves of Italian, Irish and Chinese immigrants, and almost every large economic power has attracted large groups of people from less prosperous nations. What we are witnessing in the 21st century, though, is different. Increasingly, people do not consider themselves leaving so much as moving. Identity is less bound by where someone comes from. We live in a world where the job you do doesn't necessarily make money for, or have value to, the country you live in (which is why Europe hates on Google so much). On top of this, skilled professionals are increasingly internationally mobile. Supported by international businesses, they have their visas sponsored anywhere in the world, and they can move more easily than ever before.

There are already organic signs that this is transforming the traditional role of a state government. Online portals like Google have helped people from hundreds of countries gather knowledge and learn skills that would have been hitherto unavailable. More and more, businesses operate globally, and the network effects of very young businesses can quickly be felt outside of their country of origin. This is having powerful, disruptive ramifications that governments have only a limited and retroactive ability to respond to. Just a few years ago, for example, it was really, really hard to get a taxi in San Francisco. SF regulations set an upper bound of 1,500 cabs for the entire city, which meant that demand was high, and supply was kept artificially low. Silicon Valley startups Uber, Lyft and a few lesser-known others set up shop in a legal gray area, and provided ridesharing services that filled an increasingly gaping hole in San Francisco's transport market.

Now each company is aggressively expanding into new markets, and disrupting the indigenous taxi services in major metropolitan areas like London, Paris and Berlin. Because of a regulatory bottleneck in San Francisco, hundreds of thousands of taxi drivers around the world are having their livelihoods thrown into question by part-time drivers who would never have dreamed of applying for a taxi medallion. Just like Chaos Theory's analogy of a butterfly flapping its wings in Spain and causing a hurricane in Kansas, small changes in one place have caused vast disruption in others. Cities like New York— where grabbing a taxi has never really been a problem, and local ridesharing services would have had a hard time finding a market—are now regularly starting to see pink moustaches and black towncars pulling up on street corners.

Foreign governments are responding with their own legislation (Germany recently set an outright ban on Uber) but not in any unified, international manner. Just like with file-sharing, online gambling and prohibition, outright bans are futile in a market where the majority of people want the services being offered. International economies are increasingly subject to the tidal forces created by unique circumstances in small, technologically innovative cultural hubs like San Francisco and Tel Aviv. The globalisation of business in this sense, and the reach of businesses across borders, has profound international effects on the broader labour market. It is also requiring increased international travel for professionals and skilled individuals.

These new migrants are far wealthier than the "huddled masses" who came on ships to the US. They are more like a 'global middle class' - already well-networked internationally, and taking on less risk socially or financially when they move countries. These people are still bounded by immigration and visa laws, but are increasingly more free to travel, and to pick and choose where they settle. They bring with them their own sets of values, which by nature of their own ambitions tend to be more liberal in terms of migration. They cross-pollinate the cultures with which they interact, and instead of feeling a sense of 'belonging' to one country or another, feel more of an affinity with the big cities across the world. As mentioned before, the cultures of international cities (London, New York, Berlin, Shanghai) are becoming more similar to one another than they are to neighbouring towns in their own country. Identity is crafted by the type of place you live, rather than just its geography. This trend means that increasingly cities can harbour more foreigners of one nationality than some cities within these people's home country. At the time of writing, London has the 6th largest population of French people of any city in the world[27].

It's easy to imagine some kind of jet-set elite, but these are not all well-heeled millionaires. Neither are they typically poor. They could be graduates fresh out of university

---

27   http://goo.gl/MZCujl - BBC News: London, France's sixth biggest city (2012)

working for engineering, pharmaceutical, consulting, banking or technology companies. They could be young or older families with two spouses from different countries; young professional couples, moving for better job opportunities. Increased mobility thanks to cheaper and more convenient international transport; international business growth and disruption at the speed of the Internet; better connectedness due to social networks and globalised news and communications; a decreasing reliance on your home country to provide gainful employment - All of these factors are slowly loosening our association of state with identity, and the freedom they give us mean that we can use a hitherto unavailable breadth of experience to work out how we want to identify ourselves. Maybe you really can choose to be 'from the city'; maybe you can choose to not really be 'from' anywhere. To stay relevant, and to serve the cities and citizens outside of the tight global orbit of "Global Cities" like San Francisco, governments are faced with a difficult choice. Redistribute wealth and power away from these hubs, at the risk of blunting 'national' economic success, or risk a decline into irrelevance, as our cities and companies begin to shape the world in their own image. This may be the shift that forces previously repressive countries into more liberal policy.

There are reasons to be cheerful about our freedom to move, and to identify ourselves on our own terms. Not everyone, though, is content to let socio-economic change take its course. At the bleeding edge there are entrepreneurs and would-be leaders who are attempting to fashion the technology to physically live outside of established countries today. There are seasteading communities, for example, who want to build floating societies, and others who want to reclaim land for new, more libertarian societies. Others are seeking to actively decentralise state powers from the inside; promoting the use of currencies like Bitcoin that are independent of state intervention. Elsewhere, states themselves are experimenting with charter cities; giving specific areas special laws to maximise economic value, or setting them up overseas to ensure the efficient spending of aid. Special Economic Zones - like Shanghai or Hong Kong - represent one extremely financially successful way in which a country has decentralised. China has created different laws for different parts of its country; ones which are optimised for stability and financial benefit.

One interesting finding that comes from research undertaken in the book The Spirit Level is that of the wealthy countries surveyed, smaller nations - city states like Singapore - are outliers in terms of having high wealth disparity, but a higher standard of education & healthcare, and lower incidence of crime. The authors explicitly call it out as an anomaly. A lot of the ideas in this book are be based around the idea that loosely affiliated bunches of smaller communities - more like big cities than small states - are better models for happiness than sprawling countries governed by by one centralised power. They are more responsive to the needs of minorities, they have less capacity to do damage (smaller armies), and it is harder for them to restrict their members from leaving.

Borders are arbitrary in that they are decided by wars and

diplomacy between neighbours, rather than any objective right of a state to land. And these are not all old wars or old agreements; South Sudan, for example became an independent state in July 2011.

Kurdistan is not a unified region], but before World War I neither was Iraq, Syria, Lebanon, Palestine/Israel, Jordan, or the Arabian Peninsula states. These states, which dominate the current geopolitical map of the Middle East, are modern Western creations.[28]

The exercise of border control has no inherent legitimacy, but it creates its own sense of identity by excluding what is outside as 'other', frequently an 'other' to be feared or mistrusted. Restricting our travel, and negating the ability of an individual to 'opt-out' of citizenship by going somewhere else, places constrictions on our physical and ideological freedom; it forces us to conform. It's important to remember that these structure exists because of their legacy and because they are enforced, not because anyone has proven that they are the best way of doing things. As former Apple CEO Steve Jobs said during a famous commencement speech at Stanford University:

Don't be trapped by dogma — which is living with the results of other people's thinking. Don't let the noise of others' opinions drown out your own inner voice.

---

28   Culcasi 'Locating Kurdistan: Contextualizing the Region's Ambiguous Boundaries' in Diener & Hagen (Rowman & Littlefield 2010) Borderlines and Borderlands: Political Oddities at the Edge of the Nation-State Pg. 117

Defining an identity which is independent, true to ourselves, and which celebrates Difference, is not only theoretically possible, it is happening. Moreover, recognising Difference and challenging dogma - being nonconformist - is essential if we want to be happy in our own skin. It helps us challenge oppressive ideas. It helps us learn from others rather than being taught to reject them, and it helps us empathise with others, which avoids conflict and contributes to everyone's happiness.

Large countries with larger centralised governments fear losing power. They react against attempts for small groups to live differently - crush gay rights protests and imprison radical thinkers. However, the increasingly disruptive forces of Internet-based businesses are challenging a state's ability to control. International migration, the globalisation of media and telecommunication networks, and the growth of online communities are all helping to erode the authority of any one authority's unquestionable opinion.

Some describe the opportunities offered by extricating oneself from these systems as "[r]isky freedoms"[29] and believe that "[p]eople may suffer from being released from their national containment, especially if it disrupts social bonds without replacing them with something new."[30] These arguments, though, seem to react against freedom on the basis that people can't take care of themselves; that

---

29   Mau (Routledge 2012) Social Transnationalism: Lifeworlds beyond the nation-state Pg. 29

30   Ibid.

they can't decide on what 'new' identity they would want other than that crafted for them by the state. Others are more positive and poetic in their description:

...a form of nomadism [is] developing. Mobility signals individualization, release from societal constraints, and new realms of individual action...the individual takes more and more control of his or her own biography...they are now able to choose the cities and, increasingly, countries where they live and to which they pay allegiance.[31]

The most important thing has to be that we get to choose how we live and what we believe. We may agree with what our government tells us, but dissent should be encouraged, rather than suppressed.

Who you are starts with who you think you are. Next time someone asks you 'where you're from' take a second to think about how you answer the question.

---

31   Mau (Routledge 2012) Social Transnationalism: Lifeworlds beyond the nation-state Pg. 63

Beyond 'Beyond Good and Evil'

Recognise the one truth - that there is no one truth. In a world of billions Happiness requires empathy rather than exclusion. Everyone's desires and beliefs are Different, but not opposed.

When we disagree with someone we can usually work the issue out between ourselves. We might reach an agreement, we might compromise, or we might just agree to disagree and get on with our lives. Some things, like which Power Ranger was the most badass, just aren't worth getting worked up over (it's the Green one, incidentally). Sometimes, though, when something serious happens, we can't just 'work it out'. Someone might have rear-ended our car, or cut down a tree and crushed our garden shed, or asked for custody of our child in a divorce hearing, and we can't agree on who is responsible or what to do. In this case, we rely on our society to sort the problem out. It's why we established laws, and it's one of the main reasons we like to be part of a society.

We find comfort in binary opposites like Good & Evil, Right & Wrong or Black & White - they're easy to understand, easy to explain, and they make decision-making easier.

The core of most of our children's stories is a fight between clearly demarcated heroes and villains, but as we grow up we realise that the world is not that simple. We have to make difficult decisions with no right answer, like whether we're comfortable with a friend having an affair. We have to make compromises with our loved ones - like moving cities or leaving jobs we love - so that we can be happy together. Our governments wrestle with larger decisions where, no matter what they do, there will be far reaching consequences both good and bad. They take horrific actions with a belief that the means justify the end - like dropping bombs on Hiroshima and Nagasaki; killing hundreds of thousands of people instantly to end war with Japan.

As members of society and as governments we have law as a crutch. The law tells us what is right and what is wrong, but it can never keep up with the new and nuanced situations that human beings encounter. The first-time someone synthesised LSD there was no law saying whether or not people should be able to use it. The first time Google put its self-driving car on the road there was no law explaining who was responsible if it crashed. Laws help create order because they give us shared values, but they cannot tell us what is right. Laws were made by people, and every single person has a different understanding of what is right and what is wrong.

Recognising that there can be no one 'right' way of doing things - that people will never want and believe the same thing, and that what we want changes over time - is core to realizing that empathy is just as necessary as a rule of law.

To live happy and fulfilled lives as a community of individuals, we have to understand that other people have different needs, and use law and enforcement not as a cookie-cutter person-maker, but as a crutch to lean on when we need to - when other people's desires are not just different, but harmful to our own.

Made to be broken

Most people think that laws are a good thing. They're quite happy that it's against the law to kill people, and they don't mind the prospect of being punished for murder if it means they won't get murdered. In obeying laws we sacrifice always being able to do what we think is right, for the security and order that comes with knowing that other people won't act on similar urges, and take our money or possessions for their own ends.

Law is a recognition that we have shared values. It's also a recognition that - although we might not always agree - we'd rather be able to resolve things in a way that minimises discomfort or damage to our society. Unfortunately humans are complicated, and the complexity of human society is nuanced to such a degree that not everything in our lives can be governed by one agreed set of statutes. Every situation is unique because cultural norms change over time, and new inventions and lifestyles change what we see as fair or right. This chapter asks you to accept that as far as human relations are concerned, there is no absolute 'right' way of doing things. Our happiness is dependent on an acknowledgment that right and wrong can only ever be a point of view, and that what we should optimise for is an approach to right and wrong that maximises our freedom to be who we want to be, rather than one which optimises for order, and forces people to conform at the cost of their individuality. Given that being 'good' is a moral choice that each of us makes, if we take away someone's ability to do what they think is right or wrong, we negate their humanity. A society of people who cannot choose to be immoral is one that can never take a moral act. Like Huxley's Brave New World, when we're deprived of adversity and the diversity that comes from discovery, existence ceases to have meaning,

Any law which can be enforced limits your personal freedom. These limits, though, are not always a bad thing. The law that makes drunk-driving illegal, for example, saves thousands of lives a year. Some laws we call 'rights' - like the right to a fair trial. In fact, rights are very similar to laws, they're just the laws that we place on governments, and the bodies that enforce the law. They are laws that say, "The government can't indefinitely put you in jail without some evidence that you've broken a law".

A law can only be a law if we think it could be enforced upon us. If there was no prospect of punishment, then obeying it would just be a personal, moral choice. The possibility of retribution or punishment - some consequence for breaking it - is an integral part of laws.

A law is a rule that the majority of people will obey. A society where no-one can be prevented from disobeying the law - and where there is no punishment for doing so - is toothless, and the laws have very little meaning.

A law that no-one will obey has no value. If it isn't enforced it isn't really a law, and if it is enforced but no-one obeys it then the whole society would be locked up, or under constant punishment.

A law is not something that gives you the 'right' to do something; like be a homosexual or go out on the streets after 10:30pm. In a society with no laws at all there would be no limitation whatsoever on what you could do; no-one gives you the 'right' to breathe or the 'right' to climb a hill.

But the world seems different when you realise that all of the laws that are imposed are laws that limit the scope of what you are allowed to do within a society. A law that says you have to pay road tax, for example, exists to limit your ability to use the roads if you haven't paid a fee. Laws that say 'you have a right to live without racial, verbal or physical abuse' exist to limit the freedoms of other people in abusing you. These limits are not necessarily 'bad' if they make for a happier, more empowered society, but they are still limits that we could break, but that we obey.

Do unto others

Although laws sometimes feel like they are set in stone (which maybe comes from Judaism, where they actually were when Moses brought them down from the mountain), in the real world they are very fluid things. No laws are here to stay forever, all countries have different laws, and those laws change over time. Prohibition of alcohol in America was introduced, and then repealed in the early

20th century. It used to be legal to drink in public spaces in the UK, but is now prohibited in many places. At the extreme end, Jim Crow laws in the USA forced segregation by law of black and white people in education and social situations, and we now generally acknowledge that as wrong.

Governments enforce new laws, and repeal restrictions they used to claim were necessary, as social sentiment changes through the years.

An act being 'against the law' doesn't mean you physically can't do it, just that there could be unpleasant consequences if you do. in fact, if a state actually manages to prohibit you from doing something, it doesn't matter whether it's illegal or not, and in fact doesn't make sense for it to be classed 'illegal' because there is no question of 'breaking' the law. Imagine if the UK government now made it illegal for people to put rubbish in the bins on London Underground platforms, in order to reduce the opportunity for opportunistic terrorist attacks. Well, in fact the government already removed all the bins, so this law, if instituted, would be meaningless, as no-one could break it anyway.

The gradual reduction of people's capacity to do things is the insidious slope to totalitarianism that Orwell recognises in 1984, where the only crime is 'thoughtcrime' - rebellious thoughts being the only thing that the state cannot control. The best way of thinking of a law is as a rule where punishment can be exacted for contravening it. Law enforcement, though, is a more subtle business than just having the brute force to punish people who break the law.

For a law to be a law it's very important that people will accept and obey it, because if they won't it can't really be enforced in the long-term. Imagine the US government passed a law banning clothes outdoors. In Winter, and outside of San Francisco's Castro district, it's very unlikely that anyone would obey that law, and if everyone decided to wear clothes anyway it would be impossible for any existing police force or a government to make them take them off, or to punish them for doing so. There just aren't enough police officers, or prison cells, and people wouldn't understand why it was necessary. It's impractical to enforce.

But getting people to obey a law doesn't mean there has to be a police officer there to punish people if they break it, or even that it has to be able to be enforced. Think about the illegal downloading of music and films. In the 2000s huge numbers of people were illegally downloading large amounts of film and music. CDs and DVDs were expensive, it was hard to purchase the content legally online, and it was almost unthinkable that you would be caught and fined for illegally downloading. All of this meant that 'piracy' or illegal downloading, became an attractive option, and many people did it. In the last few years, though, there have been far fewer people illegally downloading files. The reason is that buying music and movies online is now far easier, and a lot cheaper price. It's still incredibly unlikely that you would get caught or fined for illegally downloading movies for free, but because there's an easy, inexpensive and legal alternative, people will obey it. There are also network effects - with a reduction in the number of people that you know illegally downloading comes a perceived risk that you are more likely to be 'picked out of the crowd' and caught.

In fact, most laws rely on the fact that almost everyone thinks that obeying it is 'better' than not obeying it. 'Better' means that the person thinks it is in their best interests. For example, most people will obey traffic lights even if there's no immediate danger (no cars around), if there's an almost non-existent chance of them being arrested and punished, and despite the fact that they could get where they were going quicker if they crossed on red. In this case it's because people believe fundamentally that having traffic lights, and not having each person who gets to the crossing make an individual judgment call, is the right thing to do; i.e. the safest and best for them overall. They think that their day-to-day life, and that of those around them, would be more chaotic and dangerous if each person was responsible for deciding, and the law wasn't there.

This doesn't mean that all laws are obeyed because people think they make sense. If we look repressive regimes, like Russia during its civil war - where farmers had their supplies taken by decree and were left to starve - people within Russia didn't necessarily understand the philosophy or logic behind the expropriation of their property or produce, and many definitely didn't agree with it, as it left them and their families to die of malnutrition. This wasn't sustainable. Farmers were killed or left to die, and so there was no reason for people to farm, and no production. However, people were forced to obey, showing that laws are sometimes enforceable because citizens are forced into a choice between two unpleasant alternatives; in this case immediate death or giving up their livelihood.

Laws are enforced using some level of complicity (agreement that obeying is in one's interests), fear (of a punishment if one breaks the law, or chaos if no-one obeys the laws) and coercion (violence, imprisonment or some other punishment if one breaks the law). Complicity is the best way to legislate if we want to maximise peoples' happiness. It means that people feel happy about the system they are a part of and that broadly it is doing 'what is right'. It also means that they don't feel like their freedom to live and be themselves is too severely restricted. For legislation that is too complex for most people to be expected to understand, like the regulation of chemical compounds in drugs, complicity is what generates trust, and lets us put our faith in experts who we are confident can represent our best interests.

Moral absolutes

A more difficult question is whether there can be objective, or absolute laws; things which are always right or wrong, and which we should legislate for or against on that basis.

Most mainstream religions teach that there is an objective moral code; something like the ten commandments (thou shalt not kill, thou shalt not steal etc.). Back in the day claiming a God told us what the right thing to do was was a convincing way to justify laws, and religious legal strictures are in fact the basis of many modern legal systems. Even if you're not religious, there's a good chance there are some things that you think are essentially wrong, and which by extension should be illegal. Paedophilia is a common example; it's hard to argue that it's ever ok.

Within religious texts, though, and throughout history, these fundamental laws are broken. The old testament, for example, condones the stoning of people until death, "eye for eye" justice systems tolerated vengeance killings in the Anglo-Saxon period. As of the writing of this book the death penalty is still in place in 32 US states.

The justification for breaking these fundamental 'ten commandment' style rules is that the world is relative, that there are some times when they have to broken for a greater good. Things in the real world are rarely this black and white though, and humans are often forced to choose between a lesser of two evils. Sometimes - almost always in fact - a trade-off happens, and for the right that you believe that you are doing, something you would consider wrong also happens.

Homicide - the killing of one human being by another - is an example we're frequently presented with. Most people generally consider killing other people to be wrong, so we could take this as an objective law. Imagine, though, if a police marksman is part of a siege during a hostage-taking. The hostage-taker is about to execute a civilian, and the marksman has a clear shot. It's the only way he can stop the mass murder - would you say that he should not do it because it was objectively wrong; that it would be better for the marksman to wait until the hostage taker had executed all the hostages before breaking in and arresting him?

What if one of the hostages secretly had a gun, and could stop the murder of ten others by killing the hostage taker. Should he hold back from doing this? Why?

Would your opinion change if there were three hundred people being held hostage by a terrorist on a plane, and the terrorist had to be killed to be stopped? Would it change if instead of hostages a kidnapper was was about to kill your children? In these situations, could you really say it was 'wrong' to kill the kidnapper or terrorist, and that because it was 'wrong' you should let the hundreds of innocent people, or the children, die?

If you do believe in objective laws - that some things are 'just wrong' - you should ask yourself on whose authority they are wrong. If it is just your own gut feeling, or the teachings of your religion, then you have to empathise; know that this is just one opinion, and that other people think different things to you. Realise that your opinions are only based on your own experience, and that those opinions change from time to time. Even the teachings of most religions have changed significantly since their inception. You have probably, at some point, realised that something you believed was incorrect, and changed your behaviour.

If you believe in objective laws because it's the way of the world - that people have always thought this - then you might consider that large groups of people can also be wrong; that lots of practices that we now 'realise' are wrong - like slavery, or the persecution of the Jews - existed in multiple societies for many hundreds of years. As the world changes, our perceptions of right and wrong also change.

And if you believe that some things are inherently 'against nature' and will always be wrong, you are expressing a belief, a gut feeling not based in on evidence. That doesn't mean it isn't valid, but it is a viewpoint based on limited interaction with people you know and your surroundings. Rape and paedophilia are often brought up as examples of things that are 'just wrong', but it's naive to say they are 'against nature'; both are practices that occur amongst other members of the animal kingdom[32] to enforce supremacy and order. Are animals 'just wrong'?

If we can agree that the laws we make and keep in our societies are artificial (that they are thought up by individuals or groups and based on belief and limited experience), and that they are enforced through a mixture of complicity, fear and coercion, then we can treat them dispassionately. In this light laws are a shared frame of mind or point of reference, rather than universal rules handed down by God. This helps us. It means we can question why we have the laws that we currently have, and also gives us the breadth of thought to imagine more fluid systems that require less fear and coercion, and can recognise that different people want different ways of living. Having laws that you think are right, rather than obeying them because you are scared of being punished, seems like a better way of doing things.

Who says?

---

32   http://goo.gl/l51ndN - Wikipedia: Animal sexual behaviour

The first question is to ask why we have the system of law that we have, and whether finds the right balance of maintaining order, whilst not restricting people's ability to be different and happy.

Laws generally come into existence due to some incident - or foreseeable incident - that a ruling government thinks is undesirable, or needs to be controlled. A law is then proposed, passed and enforced. Drink-driving is an obvious example of an incident causing 'undesirable' consequences; car-crashes were happening whilst people were driving drunk, so the government made it illegal to drive whilst drunk. We know that not everyone obeys this law, but it is generally obeyed because of the three reasons we mentioned before, that a) a lot of people agree drink-driving is dangerous to themselves and others, b) harsh punishments are given to many people who drink and drive, and c) people know this and so do not drink-drive for fear of imprisonment. Limits on importing and exporting goods are good examples of laws that are imposed due to foreseeably undesirable circumstances. During the outbreak of mad cow disease in the 90s the EU commission, believing that exporting British beef could spread the disease to continental Europe, made the movement of British beef across borders illegal.

So far, so sensible. Often, though, laws are imposed without forethought, due to a 'knee-jerk' reaction; a perceived need to take immediate action to solve an immediate problem. Sometimes, as in the case of vCJD, these seem reasonable. Other times they are excessive, restrictive, and damaging to people's happiness.

The Stop Online Piracy Act (SOPA) in the US is a good example. It was introduced in the House of Representatives in the US in 2011, and has been heavily debated and protested. Against the backdrop of massive online piracy, and heavy lobbying pressure from the entertainment industry, SOPA was introduced to expand the ability of U.S. law enforcement to fight online piracy and theft of intellectual property. Amongst other things, what it sought were court orders that banned search engines from linking to offending sites, and to stop internet service providers from allowing access to sites. These were limitations imposed on the freedoms of private companies and, indirectly, what individual people were able to find online. Whilst we may believe that the piracy of content is wrong, making it illegal for companies to provide links to sites that could be used legally seems a heavy-handed way of dealing with a problem. It restricts more freedom than necessary, and shuts down access to information at the same time as it blocks access to piracy. In this case public and corporate protest prevailed, and the legislators backed down.

Minimising how much our freedoms are limited should be the major consideration when legislating. It doesn't seem right to stop large numbers people from doing things which are innocuous, fun, or just plain normal, because a tiny minority use that freedom to cause problems. It's the difference between punishing people who drink-drive, and banning alcohol entirely. It's like banning chocolate because some people eat too much and get fat.

In this light SOPA becomes doubly troubling. The law was titled in such an ambiguous and open-ended way as to allow broad and far-reaching enactment of the law beyond the original proposed purpose. The full and official title of SOPA is as follows:

To promote prosperity, creativity, entrepreneurship, and innovation by combating the theft of U.S. property, and for other purposes.[33]

Those last four words are weasel words, and they should give you no small degree of concern. The first time I read them I laughed; it was a bit like someone saying, "I'm buying a gun so I can do target practice, protect my home and...errr...some other stuff too." In those last four words, "and for other purposes" the government is given free reign to ban sites from search engines, or from the list of "allowed" websites to which ISPs can link. If you were cynical (like me) then you might think that "other purposes" could extend to websites that criticise the government, or which promote dissident thought, or literally anything else. Because this is exactly how they're used in China, or Russia, or North Korea (if North Korea even needs to write its restrictive laws down).

In this case legislation was drafted, introduced and promoted as a reaction and solution to a current problem in such a deliberately vague way as to allow for wide-ranging abuses of freedom that are unrelated to the initial problem. The clause is right there, on its own, at the end - they didn't

---

33   http://goo.gl/f1SKpl - Wikipedia: Stop Online Piracy Act

even bother to make it a core part of the goal for SOPA. At the very least we can see that the law is a very dangerous tool for solving problems within a society. It's a bit like using a rocket launcher to kill a mosquito.

Another reason that laws 'are the way they are' is through inertia. Many laws have existed for a long time, and although they no longer make sense in the same way they once did, they've never been repealed because they are beneficial to the state, and are difficult for a population to protest against.

One peculiar example is income tax in the UK. Tax is something most of us pay (grudgingly) because we understand that it goes to services like healthcare, law enforcement, building our roads and helping the poor. But income tax in the UK originally had nothing to do with any of this. A world without tax may seem unimaginable now, but its path to mainstream acceptance (at least in the UK) was not steady, and faced fierce opposition over the years. Time for a history lesson!

Income tax was introduced in December 1798, under William Putt the Younger, to pay for weapons and equipment in preparation for the Napoleonic Wars. In the 50 years that followed - under Addington and then Sir Robert Peel - the tax was abolished, but then renewed. It was promised to that it would be maintained on only a short-term basis, with the claim that it was needed to shore up an empty exchequer and a growing deficit.

By 1847 it was still in effect, and at the 1847 general

election Disraeli and Gladstone both promised to repeal income tax. Disraeli won, but the the tax stayed. In introducing the 1853 budget, Gladstone outlined plans for phasing out income tax over seven years, but it didn't happen. In 1868 Disraeli was elected Prime Minister. Income tax was maintained throughout his first Government, but he publicly reinforced a determination to end it. Disraeli won the election, but again, the tax remained. The government claimed that with worsening trade conditions, including the decline of agriculture as a result of poor harvests, it was still needed. Although there have been changes to the way income tax is imposed, and the rates charged to different levels of salary, its repeal has never since been seriously challenged.

Whether or not we believe income tax is good or bad, we can see that law and rules become part of the public consciousness through inertia and necessity rather than because people agree with them. Here we have a law that was introduced as a short-term answer to funding a war, and which was maintained because it provided funding to a government whose spending was growing beyond its means. Using the fear of external crises (the Crimean War) and financial problems for the government, the promise of repeal was reneged upon for so long that a new generation had grown up in a UK that had never been without income tax. Having never lived in a world without income tax, the new generation had far less reason to question it, and because it was and is so hard to disobey (in the UK income tax is automagically deducted before you get paid it is very hard to protest.

These laws do not just persist because of inertia. They persist because once institutionalised they become very hard to protest and repeal. More often than not, governments are willing to disregard a rational or popular voice because a law is convenient or lucrative. It helps to solidify or consolidate the power of that state, which those in power convince themselves is good for the country. States will go to great effort to maintain these powers once gained, which is why a mentality of nonconformism and protest is so important. Prevention is better than the cure.

An exploration of how 'knee-jerk' legislation persists and can be abused would not be complete without mentioning the USA PATRIOT act. Introduced in the wake of the September 11th terrorist attacks, the stated purpose of the act was to "deter and punish American terrorists in the United States and around the world, to enhance law enforcement investigatory tools, and for other purposes". The italics are mine, but hopefully you noted those last four weasel words again.

The US government capitalised on a state of fear and uncertainty after the terrorist attacks, and passed this law very quickly. Much high profile literature and commentary has been made on the lack of attention given to the bill[34], and as we can see in the trailing "...and for other purposes", it uses the same vague definition as SOPA in order to allow use for purposes other than anti-terrorism. Similarly to the story of income tax, the law was passed

---

34   Perhaps the most high profile being Michael Moore's 2004 film Fahrenheit 9/11

with a promise that many of the limitations it placed on freedom would be curtailed at a set date. This date was reached in 2005, at which point the provisions of the law were prolonged indefinitely. Some aspects have been struck down as unconstitutional, but many have been maintained. The 'tools' that it allowed included the following things (again, I added indignant italics):

- Allowing the government to force Internet Service Providers to include not only "the name, address, local and long distance telephone toll billing records, telephone number or other subscriber number or identity, and length of service of a subscriber" but also session times and durations, types of services used, communication device address information (e.g. IP addresses), payment method and bank account and credit card numbers of individuals.
- A provision that allows the FBI to make an order for any tangible things (including books, records, papers, documents, and other items) for an investigation to protect against international terrorism or clandestine intelligence activities.
- Allowing the government to secretly request and obtain library records for large numbers of individuals without any reason to believe they are involved in illegal activity.
- Demand letters called "National Security Letters" issued to a particular entity or organization to turn over various records and data pertaining to individuals. They require no probable cause or judicial oversight and also contain a gag order, preventing the recipient of the letter from disclosing that the letter was ever issued.

Due to its controversial nature, a number of bills were

proposed to amend the USA PATRIOT Act. These included the Protecting the Rights of Individuals Act, the Benjamin Franklin True Patriot Act, and the Security and Freedom Ensured Act (SAFE). None were passed.

Again, whether or not the laws within the PATRIOT Act were necessary (and US courts themselves have struck down many of them), we can see that a complex series of laws were introduced as a knee-jerk reaction, perpetuated under the claim of being necessary to 'protect citizens', whilst at the same time hugely marginalising individual freedoms. These powers were defended and consolidated to give the government sweeping powers to intrude on people's lives, and seize their private records and possessions, secretly and without any need for evidence of lawbreaking. These powers could be exercised with impunity and no accountability.

They may seem extreme, but these examples are now at the heart of the legal systems of what are considered some of the most 'free' nations in the world. They demonstrate that laws have powerful and far-reaching consequences on our lives, our freedom, and the lives of our children. The fact that in many cases just one one specific and isolated incident led to a law being passed indefinitely should help us to realise that we place our faith in legislation rather than public opinion at great cost.

A famous and celebrated quotation from Benjamin Franklin is that "They who can give up essential liberty to obtain a little temporary safety, deserve neither liberty nor safety." The essence of this statement is that 'essential liberty' - the ability to exercise your will as you would wish - is the only real security on which we can rely, and that giving up any of those freedoms in exchange for alleged protection allows entry onto a slow road to oppression. There are analogues in almost all of the great historical totalitarian regimes; perhaps the most striking being the creeping, 'salami-slice' way in which Jewish people were oppressed in NAZI Germany.

Prevention is better than the cure - protesting and advocating against restricting rights and freedoms is much easier than protesting to get them back. Once a Free Press has been removed in a country, what broadcast media will be used to campaign for its return? If access to Social Networks has been illegalised and restricted, and mobile networks are being surveilled, how can large groups of protesters organise themselves?

Freedom from, Freedom to

Some laws create incursions into our freedom and privacy that far overreach the problem they are introduced to solve. Others, though, seem to impose limitations that solve no problem at all. These create what we call 'victimless crimes'.

One example is the illegalisation of drugs like cannabis and MDMA in the UK. They remain illegal despite the fact that far more damaging and addictive substances like tobacco and alcohol can be bought over the counter, and that using them is far less harmful to the people around us. If I was at home - alone - would it be harmful to anyone else if I chose to smoke pot that I'd grown in my garden? If I was with friends at a party and took MDMA, would it be dangerous to anyone who hadn't consented? Would it be more or less dangerous than getting blind drunk in a pub, which is completely legal.

Drugs are a thorny issue. The lack of understanding about the damaging effects of alcohol and tobacco before their widespread use (compared to our knowledge of the effects of cannabis and MDMA), has led to double standards, where some drugs are legal, despite being more harmful and more addictive than others. It has also created a world where purchasing drugs can indirectly harm other people by funding gangs that also deal in weapons and people trafficking. It is not a perfect analogy for the 'victimless' crime.

As societies, our approach to actions which can cause self-harm is often to regulate them, and to legislate against them. We tax fatty foods, and we ban drugs as soon as they are synthesised. But self-harm is inherently a subjective thing. Is drinking a glass of wine at dinner and killing brain cells harming yourself? What about smoking cigarettes a day and giving yourself lung cancer? Is rock climbing and breaking your leg harming yourself? Our right to treat our own bodies how we want to is one of the fundamental parts of our free will, and it's one of the areas where it becomes clearest that laws should be a crutch we fall back on in extreme circumstances, rather than a barrier we use to stop people doing what they want to.

*   *   *

If I want to eat fatty foods that are 'bad' for me, is it right for the government to make them illegal?

If you eat too much chocolate and other fatty foods without exercising you will get fat, and this carries risks to your health, like diabetes and heart disease. You know this isn't necessarily 'good for you', but there are trade-offs that you enjoy (like getting to eat whatever you want). Should a government be able to make it illegal for me to eat chocolate? En masse, lots of people eating these foods and getting unhealthy will raise the costs of healthcare, so you could say it's in everyone's best interests to ban fatty foods. Maybe, though, there's a better way of organizing things. Maybe we should give people the freedom to eat what they want, but ask them to take responsibility for their diet and lifestyle choices. Medical insurance companies already charge extra to people who smoke, overeat or drink excessively, and it seems a more fair and free way of doing things to tell people the risks, let them choose, but ask them to be responsible for decisions they know could be harmful. We do the same with waivers for extreme sport and other high-risk activities.

If I want to take cocaine every day, should that be illegal?

Cocaine is highly addictive, and has physically damaging side effects. However, most people who take cocaine are fully aware of this. The high street price of this and other drugs - which often leads to users turning to crime to maintaining a habit - is because the drug is illegal. Likewise, a lot of the physical damage is caused by impurities with which the drug is cut before it is sold. This happens because production is illegal, and therefore not regulated. If there was no law against cocaine sale or consumption, we would have a far lower price, and because a society would be able to regulate the sale, a much purer, safer form of the drug sold by reputable companies. Should it be illegal? Should alcohol and tobacco be illegal?

If I want someone else to hurt me, should that be illegal?

Most countries have laws to prevent people from hurting others. If you went to a bar and smashed a bottle of whisky over someone's head, you'd probably be arrested. Sometimes, though - and let's be honest for a second - we do get pleasure from other people hurting. Often this is fairly innocuous sexual foreplay, like biting or scratching. For some people, though, it involves violent acts - things like whipping or asphyxiation. This enters the realm of BDSM, and maybe conjures up stereotypical images of kinky sex dungeons and leather. If it makes the sex better, it makes me and my partner happier, and we both fully consent to the acts being performed, is it really that bad? Just like hang-gliding or eating fatty foods, I've made a decision, aware of the physical harm, but decided that it's worth it.

Some people think this sexual violence is 'bad for society', and that it gives the wrong message to others. Some people are against homosexuality for precisely the same reasons.

If I am suffering from a terminal, incurable and painful disease and want to die, should it be illegal for someone to kill me?

Euthanasia is controversial, and every case has unique factors. Arguments against euthanasia often include the patient not being 'sound mind', self-interest or conspiracy on the part of friends or family (if they are pursuing an inheritance etc.), or religious and moral objections.

England, 2002. Dianne Pretty, a long-suffering motor-neurone disease patient, dies after slipping into a coma. Dianne was of 'sound mind', and wanted to die. She and her husband petitioned the courts to give immunity from prosecution to him if he were to help her kill herself, but this was denied. She endured immense pain and debilitating suffering, and died in hospital under exactly the sort of conditions she had wanted to avoid.

In society we generally say that killing other people is wrong. Here, a hospital patient is of sound mind but paralysed, suffering an incurable and painful disease. It seems inhumane to make an act of euthanasia - killing this woman - illegal. Instead, we condemn someone to a slow, painful death in paralysis, and you have to wonder what has been gained.

If I consent to be killed and eaten by someone else, should that be illegal?

A more disturbing topic. Cannibalism has been historically viewed with distaste (forgive the pun) by many societies.

However, in 2003 Germany witnessed one of its more extraordinary legal cases. Armin Meiwes killed, cooked and ate his friend Bernd Brandes. Brandes had been recorded on video consenting to this beforehand and, after Brandes had consumed a considerable volume of drugs and sleeping pills, Meiwes cut off Brandes' penis, which the two cooked and ate together before Meiwes stabbed Brandes in the neck. As cannibalism was not classified as illegal in Germany, Meiwes was charged with murder for the purposes of sexual pleasure and with "disturbing the peace of the dead". He was eventually found guilty of manslaughter, but we have to consider whether - if we agree that euthanasia and participation in violent BDSM - we should classify what Meiwes did as illegal. He assisted in the killing of a man who wanted to be killed, and the violence that Meiwes inflicted upon Brandes was fully consensual. Both men wanted what happened to happen.

It is too reductive to classify both parties "insane" just because their desires were very unconventional, and it is dangerously recursive to be able to label people "insane" just for doing things that are illegal. The range of human desires is extremely wide, and to label someone mentally ill for wanting to eat people, or wanting to be whipped for sexual pleasure, or wanting to drink themselves to death, or even for being homosexual (as happened in the UK) negates their humanity. It allows them to be sectioned, and for their individual freedoms to be taken away. It diminishes them, and allows us to treat them as though their free will is simply 'wrong'.

If I want to divorce my wife, is it right for the government to make that illegal?

We've looked at things that are physically or mentally harmful, but which people want to do because it will make them happy (or they think it will make them happy). If we feel that the government should be allowed to legislate to stop us from 'harming' ourselves, what about other actions that we take that could potentially harm us? If I am married, and decide to divorce my wife, is that ok? Divorce is psychologically damaging, with potential physical effects due to depression. Additionally, being single and alone reduces your life expectancy because there is no other half checking up on your health. Should the government make divorce illegal because it's bad for your long term health?

If I want to stop talking to people, is it right for the government to make that illegal?

And what if I just don't want to participate in society? Research has demonstrated that the long-term effects of living a solitary, antisocial life in a developed country include depression and a lower life-expectancy. Should we make it 'illegal' for people to not socialise? If we believe that the purpose of law is to protect us from self-harm, this would be the logical thing to do.

*　　　*　　　*

Thanks for bearing with that little diversion. Some of the examples were every-day, some far-fetched; some were legal, others less so. In all of them, though, we can see that normally black and white questions - like whether it's ok to kill someone - become far from simple over the course of human lives. Sometimes people do need to be prevented from harming others, and other times it is incredibly hard to tell whether the 'harm' someone received was consensual. In all cases, though, we see that just 'applying the law' is dangerous. In each of these cases the it could not capture the unique human needs. Laws are a good general guide, but empathy - and an understanding that other people have very different desires from the majority - is required to let people live the lives they want to.

These examples are not here as a preamble to advocating a society with no system of law. What they hopefully suggest, though, is that there is no cookie-cutter answer for every situation. Because different people need different things to be happy, we cause a great deal of restriction and misery by applying exactly the same laws to incredibly different people. Legal systems allow only very limited opportunity for judges to exercise discretion and empathy, and in a world where the gulf between people's perspectives on right or wrong are truly vast - where some people literally desire death at someone else's hands, whilst others believe all life is sacred - we need to rethink how a society treats its people. Not only do we unfairly punish those with extreme and unusual desires, but we also restrict the freedom of 'reasonable' men and women.

Status Quo

Some things do work well. We have speed limits & traffic light regulation at dangerous intersections. We make rape, paedophilia and torture[35] illegal because they violate and hurt innocent people. For the vast majority of people these laws require no use of punishment in order to be enforced. Most people don't do them because they truly believe that they are wrong.

Other laws that we have broadly work well, but exist within a reality where they are rarely enforced, and frequently broken. Count off which of the following you've done before:

- Underage drinking
- Underage smoking
- Taken an illegal substance
- Run a red light
- Broken the speed limit
- Parked in a no-parking zone
- Crossed the road without using a pedestrian crossing

Most people would tell you these laws 'made sense', but almost everyone has broken one of them at some point in their life. They have knowingly broken the law, but with what they would consider to be a reasonable excuse ('it was too late to stop'; 'I had to speed up to overtake'; 'I was only parked for a minute whilst I dropped someone off' or even, 'everyone else was doing it'). Most of us sympathise, even if we recognise that the law is imposed for a good reason. The way the system currently works, though, you could be punished for any of the above, even if everyone not in a uniform thinks it's actually not that bad. What if

---

35   Unless you work for the government.

there was a way of implementing such laws that does not categorically limit these freedoms, and allows some flexibility without undermining the principles. As well as giving us more personal freedom, might it also help to maintain law and order?

Let's take drugs as an example - cannabis, cocaine, ecstasy and heroin:

- Do most people believe these drugs should be illegal in the UK? It's hard to say.
- Do a significant percentage of people, including leading academic and political experts, believe some, if not all, should be legalised? Yes.
- Is current drug legislation working in the UK? It is not.
- Are illegal drugs available on the streets of the UK? Yes.
- Do people buy them and use them (knowingly disobeying the law)? Yes, in increasing numbers.
- Does this lead to an erosion of confidence in the legal system, and a lack of respect? Yes.
- Does the illegalisation of drugs raise their street price (leading to higher petty crime to pay for habits)? Does it cost millions in police money and resources to combat (leading to higher taxes), and help fund violent, repressive organisations (who funnel the money to arms and people trafficking)? Yes, yes and yes.
- Could this be avoided if drug consumption was made legal, and a consensus reached about how to regulate sales? Yes. Far less money would be spent prosecuting misuse & the associated crime, and far more money made by law-abiding companies in sales, which would reach the government through taxes.

This Q&A outlines the major problem with outlawing freedoms people enjoy. Not only will people break the law, but opportunities are created for those who would help them do it illegally. Trying to place limitations on such freedoms is difficult and expensive. It causes conflict and disunity, undermines faith in the law and enforcement, and allows people who control these illegal networks to make even more money.

Banning drugs is one thing - it's a complex issue where each of the different approaches to restriction and legalisation have positive and negative effects. Banning activities that we choose to do with our own bodies is quite another, though.

In some countries BDSM is not usually penalised, provided there is mutual consent amongst the partners involved. British law, though, does not recognise the possibility that you can consent to bodily injury. In the UK these acts are illegal - even between consenting adults - and so although London is a centre for the fetish scene, there are only very private events for the BDSM scene. Unfortunately, this knock-on effect means that the more violent and dangerous acts are forced underground. The whole system is harder to monitor, and real abuses of human rights are harder to detect. There is a famous 1987 incident, which became the case of Laskey, Jaggard and Brown v. United Kingdom[36], where the police uncovered tapes that they

---

36   http://goo.gl/bAza2l - Wikipedia: Laskey, Jaggard and Brown v United Kingdom

believed showed sado-masochistic torture, followed by the participants being murdered. The police launched a murder enquiry, and although they found all the participants alive and well - and were told that the acts were completely consensual - they still arrested the consenting individuals and pressed charges. The case went to the European commission for Human Rights, which found that "the amount of physical or psychological harm that the law allows between any two people, even consenting adults, is to be determined by the jurisdiction the individuals live in, as it is the State's responsibility to balance the concerns of public health and well-being with the amount of control a State should be allowed to exercise over its citizens." This was a cop-out, essentially saying that the UK had the right to decide to punish two people for harming each other, even if the acts were consensual.

In this case 'the state' in the form of England's House of Lords, determined that consent was not a defence to their actions. Lord Templeman made the following statement when dismissing an appeal against the decision:

In principle there is a difference between violence which is incidental and violence which is inflicted for the indulgence of cruelty. The violence of sadomasochistic encounters involves the indulgence of cruelty by sadists and the degradation of victims. Such violence is injurious to the participants and unpredictably dangerous. I am not prepared to invent a defence of consent for sadomasochistic encounters which breed and glorify cruelty [...]. Society is entitled and bound to protect itself against a cult of violence. Pleasure derived from the infliction of pain is an evil thing. Cruelty is uncivilised.

Throwing around words like "evil" is not a great way to make law. What Templeman's words emphasise are his own personal views, and a sadly dated moral perspective. His perception of cruelty, and his definition of evil, are evidently different to those willing participants. Instead of looking at whether individual freedoms were violated, or if anyone was made to do anything against their will (which is his job), he stated that the acts were categorically wrong. The men in court, having been involved in consensual but violent homosexual acts, were convicted for assault occasioning actual bodily harm.

This is not a method of creating and enforcing law that has freedom in mind. Again, punishing these men for acts that they wanted to perform - without harm to other people - forces their behaviour underground. Maybe next time a group of people indulged in this behaviour something went wrong, and someone died accidentally. Because the participants would all risk prosecution if they spoke up, it's possible they just didn't, and no-one found out about it at all. Banning consensual human behaviour makes it more difficult for the police to be involved when real acts of violation take place.

There are parallels here with the way in which self-harm, whilst not itself illegal, is prevented by a state. Self-harmers in the UK, if the harm is considered serious, are restrained under the Mental Health Act of 1983. The act allows for people diagnosed with a mental disorder to be detained in hospital or police custody, and have their disorder assessed or treated against their wishes (unofficially known as "sectioning"). The problem here is that the legal definition of mental order under the Mental Health Act is recursively vague. A mental disorder is defined as "any disorder or disability of mind" and so, in layman's terms, "a mental disorder is a mental disorder." There are only subjective bounds (to be defined by whichever authority is enforcing the law) on who should be classified with a disorder and for what reason. If we think that such legislation would not be abused we are being naive. It is used to stop people from self-harming in the UK (even though this act that is not illegal), and was used extensively in the Soviet Union[37] (and many other countries) to discredit, imprison and break the will of people with political views that differed from the state. Whatever your views on the health of self-harming, using general and vaguely-defined laws to deprive someone of their freedom for something which isn't even against the law is draconian and open to abuse (if you need convincing, watch One Flew Over the Cuckoo's Nest).

As we've seen, a lot of legislation is willfully vague in defining the grounds on which people can be arrested or detained. Where the state has an agenda the application of the law is bent by misinterpretations and subjective arguments around the 'rightness and wrongness' of the acts. These examples are neither isolated, nor necessarily extreme. In June 2012 Conservative Prime Minister of the UK, David Cameron, went on television to declare

---

37   http://goo.gl/lCgomy - Wikipedia: Political abuse of psychiatry in the Soviet Union

comedian Jimmy Carr's tax payments 'immoral' despite the fact that they were legal. He said: "Some of these schemes we have seen are quite frankly morally wrong. People work hard, they pay their taxes, they save up to go to one of his shows. They buy the tickets."

A good law requires as little interpretation as possible. Laws are not immutable, and a community who makes them must be willing to challenge them based on unique circumstances. Politicians debating the morality rather than legality of an individual's behaviour, though, are not the grounds by which people should be forced to change their lifestyles. We have laws precisely so that we don't need to rely on one person's moral judgment to work out what to do in a particular situation.

One law?

Big countries like China or the US offer some of the best examples of how one centrally enforced legal code can create problems for the lives and happiness of citizens. In rural Arkansas, where farms are isolated, and farmers have to deal with foxes attacking their chickens, it might make sense for you to own a gun. In New York City, which has a dense, urbanised population, there's a likelihood you'd do far more harm than good. As mentioned before, China has recognised that to be economically successful its big cities require different rules (at least fiscally) compared to other areas. One law for everyone isn't always in everyone's best interests, but suggesting we have different laws for different people sounds messy. It begs the questions of whether we actually do need some kind of state authority to enforce our laws.

In absolute terms the answer is no, we don't need one, but when we move away from that model things don't always go well. There are areas like Somalia, which has had no authoritative central government for a while, and where laws are administered ad-hoc by militias. Similarly, in the Democratic Republic of the Congo, where government has in reality very little law enforcement power, small paramilitary groups maintain their own rule of law through extreme violence. There are areas like Iraq (in the immediate aftermath of the second Gulf War), where private enforcement was brought in by a foreign government to maintain law according to its own values; essentially annexing it. None of these systems had the interests of the majority in mind, and each caused bloodshed, torture and humanitarian disaster.

A better question, then: is one central authority necessary in enforcing laws that most people agree with?
Again the answer is no. On a very small scale there are roving communities of nomads - like the Bedouin - who observe no borders but have a system of rules - legislation - to which their members conform. It tends to be easier to do this with small groups, as everyone knows one another, and faces exclusion if they do something wrong.

Communities like the Amish in the US are larger, but provide a socially enforced system of law and ethics without the overhead of a nation state. There is a division of labour, almost non-existent crime internally, and high social stability.

This society isn't perfect. It is insular, both geographically and culturally, and very technophobic. It allows young people the freedom to opt-out and experience a year in the outer 'real' world, to see if they want to stay within the community, but these people are often already so indoctrinated by their community to be morally against what they see out there (liberal attitudes to dress, drink, sex, drugs and gender roles) that they return out of sheer fear of the difference. Nevertheless, it is a working and cohesive society with very little organised and violent enforcement (police or military), no oversight by a nation-state, and a high level of happiness and fulfillment

Within even the largest states we observe "laws" with which the vast majority comply, but which have no formal legislation. Borrowing this example from a man called Shaffer, consider the rise of the ATM:

At the ATM people tend to stand a couple of metres behind the person using the machine, so as to allow them privacy...Those little yellow lines and boxes you sometimes see around them didn't come first, but were added to formalise an existing social convention.

Shaffer talks about the "authentic quality" of informal behaviour like this; a rule put in place for everyone's benefit and to which very few people disagree, but which has no grounding in written law. There are a million social niceties that we observe without any legal grounds or fear of arrest, and which we take part in because they make society more pleasant and less stressful for everyone (queueing for a bus, standing on one side of the escalator to let people pass etc.) Many, like talking quietly on public transport, have very limited personal benefit, short of avoiding social awkwardness. There is little fear of punishment if we contravene them, we just obey them because we think we should obey them; they maintain a status quo that we find comforting.

In looking for an actual country where where informal rules, and a strong, internalised sense of right and wrong often take away the need for enforced law, the world has one premier example: Japan. In Tokyo - one of the largest metropolitan areas in the world and one of the most diverse cities in the country - street crime is incredibly low[38] compared to that in Western countries, and the sense of politeness and common courtesy is tangible. Order exists with very little physical enforcement; people know how to behave to maintain the status quo, and they do. Japan's sense of order and propriety even extends - perversely - into the world of organised crime, where the Yakuza solidify power and influence through ownership of many public companies, like banks.

It's not all good news, though. This level of conformity, deference to authority and adherence to a dogmatic sense of right and wrong has created huge hierarchical bureaucracies that make their employees miserable. Common in Tokyo is the idea of a 'salary man'; a young to middle-aged man in a business suit who works all hours

---

38   http://goo.gl/sbsScc - Nationmaster: The secret of Japan's mysteriously low crime rate (2014)

and slaves away his youth for mediocre pay, incremental promotion over tens of years, and very little satisfaction. Japan also has an unusually mercuric approach to sexuality; notions of prudence and morality make discussions of sex, and even public displays of affection taboo, whilst 'love hotels', cinemas and other attractions cater for all manner of deviant tastes behind closed doors. It creates domestic disharmony; a surface repression between couples and families that marriages loveless, encourages mistresses and affairs, and finds its outlet in all manner of underground fetishes.

Better living through legislation?

So if everyone has different needs and desires, if our existing models for making and enforcing laws could be much better tailored to making us happy, and if there are actually ways of helping everyone get along with much less violent law-enforcement and punishment, what do we do? How do we avoid knee-jerk, vague and sweeping legislation, laws which limit freedom for no benefit, the cronyism and corruption which breeds a conservative retrenchment in legislation, and unaccountable centres of power peopled by politicians who are detached from the needs and desires of the populace? And, just as importantly, how do we do this and maintain, or increases upon, the level of individual security and happiness that we currently enjoy? How do we avoid the pitfalls of a society like Japan's, or the chaos and violent rule of somewhere like Somalia?

Most basic, and perhaps so basic that it is often

overlooked is that a system of law could be opt-in. Pretty much everything we do as human beings is the result of a choice, and when choice is denied us we feel violated. If I see a man collecting for Save the Children I have a choice as to whether I give him money or not. If I was forced to give him money every time I saw him I'd be pretty annoyed. It's the same if I was prevented from giving him money, and it's the same with most human activities; we opt in to social groups, we opt in to relationships, sports, hobbies, buying a car, and when we feel forced into doing something it makes us upset.

There are three main things in society into which we are opted in 'by default'. One is our family, and for those who are not orphaned or abandoned children, it is pretty obvious why we do not get to pick them. The second is education. We're told that the education we receive is in our interests, and as a child we're generally neither mature nor capable enough to suggest or create a better alternative. Parents rarely have the time or inclination to educate their own kids. The third is the state itself. We're born a citizen who is registered, taxed and forced to obey laws that we had no part in creating.

The arguments for mandatory citizenship is that 'opting out' is not really possible. Even if it was like Amish communities, and we were allowed to opt out upon adulthood, where would we go? Every country mandate citizenship, and there is almost no habitable land unclaimed by any state. Almost no-one has the wealth to buy islands or land from governments who would sell it, and 'owning' land within a country does not insulate you from its laws. Quite the opposite; you're reliant on a government to protect your rights as a homeowner. This is - unfortunately - a pretty strong argument. What it doesn't address are the ways in which the geographical state and the identity of a citizen are becoming increasingly unbound, and that countries will soon need to address an overwhelming number of people who want to 'opt out', over and above the small number of people who today surrender citizenship for somewhere else.

What we want above all else is consensus and empathy. Rather than ruling with fear and violence, it's better to have everyone agree with how things are done, and understand different people's needs. In this case it makes sense to start small: within a smaller group it's easier to hone in on the specific values and laws a group thinks are proper and necessary. This doesn't mean that you couldn't have a country-sized volume of people governed by one set of laws, just that the best way to start of a cohesive, successful group is with a small group of people who have similar views and desires.

However similar our values are, each person is different (different experience, gender, race, age etc.), and all of these differences mean everyone will have a different perspective, and a different way of doing things. This Difference should be celebrated rather than suppressed - different opinions and perspectives are what keep us honest; they create a society in which it's more acceptable to be non-conformist, and where there's less of a prevailing dogma. People are more empowered to challenge social wrongs that they see, and the whole group is less likely to obey one list of rules blindly. In short, it's less likely to create a totalitarian systems.

As well as celebrating diversity and letting people 'opt in' to society, any written rules really do need to be with accuracy, in language that all who have agreed to them can understand. No-one should be signing on the dotted line without knowing what they're letting themselves in for, and unfortunately we live in a world where terms of service are so sprawling and vast that we agree to them without a thought to what we're sacrificing.

If legislation is what limits our freedom, then the rule of thumb should be 'as little as possible', and it should be focused around encouraging us not to do harm others, rather than 'pre-empting' crimes. If it becomes impossible to commit an illegal act, then there is no need for legislation. In an absolute sense, if we are incapable of doing what is classed as 'wrong' (by extension of its being illegal) and it becomes impossible to have a concept of right. It might seem counterintuitive, but delegislation and deregulation often have a very positive impact on a society. Recently a number of European cities have taken to abolishing traffic signs, leaving traffic decisions to be made independently by motorists. The policy has almost invariably led to a dramatic reduction in traffic accidents.[39] In his book on the topic, Shaffer quotes an advocate of the policy:

---

39   Shaffer (Ludwig von Mises Institute 2009) Boundaries of Order: Private Property As a Social System 5%

The many rules strip us of the most important thing: the ability to be considerate. We're losing our capacity for socially responsible behaviour.[40]

The sentiment may sound rose-tinted and melodramatic, but the point is important. In a world where people must be more conscious of and responsible for the implications of their decisions - where the social stigma instead comes from doing something that is 'wrong' - people are likely to take far more care somewhere like a traffic intersection. With traffic lights and regulation, one out-of-control person could charge through a red light and cause a pile-up through the line of cars 'legally' crossing the other way on green. Without this regulation, everyone would be far more aware of their surroundings, and be better able to avoid an out-of-control motorist.

As systems become more complicated and nuanced regulation becomes necessary. In a built-up area traffic regulation becomes necessary to ensure efficiency as well as just safety, but this helps make another strong point: laws need to be built for flexibility. They need to understand and plan for moral shades of grey, and the subjective nature of 'interpreting the law'. It might be necessary to have traffic regulated by lights and enforced in a built up city area, but not in the countryside. Similarly, it may be necessary to limit the level of emissions allowed from cars within built-up areas, but not in the countryside, where pollutants dissipate in the atmosphere without directly harming people as much.

---

40   Ibid.

Hardcore believers in the free-market often look to 'market forces' as a mechanism for solving social problems:

If almost everyone believes strongly that heroin addiction is so horrible that it should not be permitted anywhere under any circumstances, anarcho-capitalist institutions will produce laws against Heroin. Laws are being produced for a market, and that is what the market wants.[41]

The problem here is that within our current states these kind of 'majority decisions' have led to a lot of the 'victimless crimes' we talked about earlier. Just because 'the market' wants to illegalise homosexuality, it doesn't mean everyone should be subjected to that perspective. Due to fear and ignorance, governments have been able to illegalise lifestyle choices like sexual orientation, and the possession of particular books (the possession of knowledge). The market can lead to the creation of laws, but not everyone within the market will be happy with them. It diminishes their happiness without rationale.

What is 'right' and what is left

So if there's no one truth, and everyone wants something different, should we just go ahead and legalise any act which doesn't directly harm another person?

---

41   Friedman 'The Machinery of Freedom' in Stringham (Transaction 2006) Anarchy and the Law: The Political Economy of Choice Pg 51.

It isn't sensible to do this all in one go, because we're not starting from a blank state. Drugs and guns are already illegal. Arms traders and drug dealers have been charging premiums on the goods they sell, and have built up strong black market networks, and a capacity for violence which they've needed to keep a competitive advantage. Instant deregulation would allow groups of violent, power-hungry people to exploit their existing networks and capitalise on the opportunity. This would likely make things a lot worse. On a more basic level, legalising something like gun ownership would put weapons in the hands of people who not only don't know how to use them, but could easily use them to murder and pillage.

People often claim that if you legalise drugs, legalise guns, get rid of speed limits, and generally pare back the laws imposed on people, then society will break down. We will have a nation of drug addicts or vigilante killers - authority will crumble and even more violent and coercive societies will emerge. We shouldn't 'legalising everything'. Instead, we should allow smaller communities - who are more united by a shared set of interests and moral values - more control over their laws and lives. We should recognise that removing rules can have just as much of a benefit to maintaining order and respect as placing them. People who are closer to one another understand each other's needs better, and if we have fewer 'rules' to hide behind, we're forced to acknowledge our Difference from one another, and accommodate it rather than suppressing it.

The last chapter gives some exciting examples of how advances in technology & communication tools, the globalisation of business, the democratisation of media and a shift in migration and living patterns makes formation of these 'smaller groups' easier, and less bounded by our location. Travel in the Eurozone has been deregulated, smart people have become far more mobile (which means governments have to liberalise to keep them), and social networks now allow oppressed groups to organise themselves physically in protest.

The same laws don't fit every situation, and not everyone has the same view of what is right or wrong. The systems we have apply blanket restrictions on all people within a country (up to the billions of people), and this has meant general laws that limit freedoms have been applied to large groups of people who disagree with them, and it makes them unhappy. What if those people were able to opt-out together, and form their own community based on a contract of shared values?

You can ask where these people would go, and it's a valid question. Almost all the land in the world is claimed by the government of one country. Furthermore, border disputes can be some of the most contentious, violent and stigmatised, as the below account of the border enclaves between India and Bangladesh demonstrates:

A politician, the chairperson of a Bangladeshi union council, was asked to arbitrate a dispute over the felling of some trees at the edge of the enclave. As soon as the chairperson and his brothers stepped into the enclave they were captured, held hostage for several days, and later killed. The Bangladeshi residents of the neighbouring communities were enraged by the brazen killing of the chairperson, the impunity of the killers in the enclave, and the inability of the Bangladeshi authorities to arrest the perpetrators. They took matters into their own hands and burned down all the houses in that enclave and drove out the residents.[42]

Some groups look to extreme solutions, like "building" new lands on the sea (seasteading); setting up floating platforms and barges to allow communities to operate outside of the law. Other options include charter cities; making an agreement with a government for a community to opt-out, or secede from the day to day laws and running of the state. Other options include extensions of these ideas; that a large private company could colonise land, reclaim it from the sea or buy it, and run it as its own corporate state; albeit a state where all the citizens-employees had opted in, and were unified under a collective set of beliefs.

Even if there isn't a silver bullet right now, it's important to realise that the systems we have at the moment - which define our aspirations, our identities, our notions of truth and our personal freedoms - can be better. The traditional ways in which people have resisted oppression can also be better. Violent revolution leads to power vacuums, a need for authority, and usually more violent, oppressive rule with one dominant dogma. Communities that celebrate

---

42   Jones 'The Border Enclaves of India and Bangladesh: The Forgotten Lands' in Diener & Hagen (Rowman & Littlefield 2010) Borderlines and Borderlands: Political Oddities at the Edge of the Nation-State Pg. 28

diversity, and which seek equilibrium through networks of shared values rather than enforced ones play to our happiness. Not only do they encourage a community having diverse aspirations, but in making it ok to want different things to other people, they make it easier for us to achieve the things we want to. That kid who was born to be a banker can still join a hedge fund, but those other kids who wanted to be sailors, or architects, or tea-traders, can do so with less pressure to conform to society's view of success; to get a degree and a good husband and a job as a management consultant. Zach Weinersmith's wonderful wordless comic Life of Thought[43] - which is reproduced here - demonstrates the joy and opportunity in Difference, and the danger of dogma.

43   http://goo.gl/lFTzUf - SMBC: Life of Thought

Room for improvement

There was no blueprint for our universe, and it was designed without the hand of any architect that we've yet been able to meet and thank. The almost infinite complexity and diversity we see around us is emergent; our galaxy, planets, mountains, trees, brains, bicycles and Pokemon games all seem to be the result of untold centillions of uncontrolled collisions; trial and error creating a semblance of order out of chaos. Because there is so much information to take in, humans have filters. We focus on the things we think have meaning, and we discard things that are irrelevant.

This focus sometimes makes us miss the bigger picture. Looking back, the story of human progress seems linear - we left the oceans, evolved from four-legged mammal to monkey to man, started tribes, settled down, built towns and cities and industry and cars and trains and planes and computers. But for every development that lasted there were far more that didn't; billions of creatures that never reproduced and passed on their genetic code; millions of people whose towns and tribes died in obscurity, thousands of once living languages now dead. Our existence seems orderly, but in fact is subject to the same chaotic experimentation and diversity that drives the evolution of our galaxies.

It's why the second boom in Silicon Valley startups has been compared to the Cambrian explosion[44] of life into the world - even though only a few will endure, overall innovation and ideas flourish where Difference is concentrated. Trial and experimentation push us forward as a species and a universe. To keep our societies healthy we have to question the established order, stress-test conventional wisdom and longstanding laws. We should always be asking whether things can be better, because they always can.

This final chapter has less structure than the others. Instead of a starting from a principle or world-view, it's more about exploring the large and small experiments that are actually happening to change our societies. Some you may be excited by, and some you might find troubling, but all of them are trying to change something they see as 'broken'. If the social status quo represents order, with the ever-present danger of authoritarianism and conformism, then human experimentation and nonconformism acts a pressure valve; a way of challenging orthodoxy and offering people an alternative. As individuals, it is the closest thing we have to a social duty to be participant in challenging dogma and experimenting. As Mark Hamill says in the computer game Wing Commander IV, "The Price of Freedom is Eternal Vigilance". At the time of

---

44   http://goo.gl/oG3a22 - Economist: A Cambrian moment (2014)

writing this book Guantanamo bay still houses 169 prisoners without trial (including some children), homosexuality is still illegal in over 70 countries, and international commissions are giving states the impunity to regulate, censor and control access to the Internet. There's a lot of work to be done.

Protecting our Privacy

Protecting our identity begins with protecting our privacy, but online and offline it's becoming increasingly difficult. A lot of people have to travel internationally for work or pleasure, and we surrender private information as a matter of course in our travels. Our streets are covered in CCTV cameras that can personally identify us, and wearing a balaclava and dark glasses out in the streets isn't really practical (trust me on that). It is estimated in the UK that there are ~1.85m cameras in public places, roughly one for every 32 people. Police forces in most countries where the technology exists are increasing the situations in which they can take biometric information from individuals - like fingerprints or saliva. Not only is that information retained indefinitely, but it is shared with other governments across the world. It may be illegal for the UK government to forcibly collect your fingerprints, but it is not forbidden for the US to share that information if they have it. You might want to consider that the next time you go through US customs.

Recent anxiety about personal information has focused on large Internet companies, like Facebook and Google, but the reality is that groups like CapitalOne, or even supermarkets like Target, have far more information about you (name, age, date of birth, nationality, Social Security number, address, phone number, bank details, marital status, family status, credit limit, previous addresses, purchase habits etc.). This information is updated every time you make a transaction, and banks cross-reference data from a variety of sources to build up detailed profiles of their customers. If you want to have a comparatively hassle-free life in a developed nation today, you have little choice but to give this information away, and it is used constantly to target you with advertising, to profile your credit risk and to pre-empt any fraud you might be thinking about engaging in.

Online it's just as difficult to safeguard privacy. Some people maintain pseudonyms online (using a username rather than their real name), but that won't keep a well-resourced government (or even a dedicated individual) from finding out your identity and correspondence. Many people - especially those in states like China where Internet access is heavily restricted - use "proxies". These are servers on the internet that mask your location and identity by routing your service through one or many other locations. **TOR**[45] **and I2P** are two of these services you might have heard of. They can be used not only to mask your identity from a government that might be tracking your activity, but also to read news and information from outside your country, which your government might have suppressed (China famously blocked Google image search results for events like the Tiananmen Square massacre,

---

45   http://goo.gl/r7Ciu3 - TOR project

and Google.cn now redirects elsewhere). If you're worried about someone watching what you're doing online, using a proxy server is a good start.

During civil unrest, governments increasingly shut down access to the Internet altogether, to prevent communication and organization. This happened recently in Syria and Egypt, and the US has its own contingency plan[46] in case of widespread public disorder. Apps like **FireChat**[47] have been developed to circumvent this, and to allow citizens peer-to-peer communication via bluetooth or 'mesh networks' which don't rely on vast cellular networks.

None of these systems are 100% secure, though, and governments have vast technical resources - and often the legal impunity - to intercept conversations for any reason they like. The most promising way to ensure we can speak confidentially is a technique called **quantum cryptography**. If you watch Star Trek you may have heard of the Heisenberg uncertainty principle, or the story of Schrödinger's Cat. The idea is that on a very, very small scale, even the act of observing something happening will have an effect on it. This means is that - using a quantum encrypted message - you can know as soon as anyone tries to intercept the call, and either stop or switch to another one. Quantum cryptography is in its infancy, but

46   http://goo.gl/JEc7is - Mother Jones: The Government's Secret Plan to Shut Off Cellphones and the Internet, Explained (2013)

47   http://goo.gl/Y5dguk - New York Times: Hong Kong Protests Propel FireChat Phone-to-Phone App (2014)

just as the Internet allowed the world hitherto unimaginable access to information across the world, quantum cryptography could give us a level of privacy upon which no-one could intrude.

And as well as communicating confidentially, cryptocurrencies like **Bitcoin** offer the opportunity to exchange money confidentially over the web. Bitcoin is a little like a Swiss Bank Account for the Internet - a platform where everyone has a unique number for their account, and can exchange money anonymously. Rather than relying on people's knowing each other, though, it is the Bitcoins (like dollars or euros) that are connected to one another, and each transaction is validated anonymously by the whole system. Bitcoin is obviously troubling for governments, as it allows people to buy and sell illegal goods anonymously, but the benefits are that the currency cannot be artificially controlled by a state, and that it's incredibly difficult for your money to be stolen, as only you have access to your unique account number.

Safeguarding knowledge

Access to information is key to learning. It helps us understand our world and other people, helps us make judgments about what is right and wrong, and gives us the depth of understanding to work out what place we want to have in the world. And access to information has exploded with the advent of the Internet. Citizen journalism, and an in international news network have all helped to keep governments visible in, if not accountable for their actions. Censorship is still rife, though, and governments across the world are constantly seeking control over what information we have access to. Communicating with each other in private is one challenge, but getting access to unbiased and uncensored news and information is quite another.

Sites like **Wikileaks** have been at the vanguard of opening up previously confidential information. They have uncovered the murder of civilians and the corrupt underside of diplomatic relations. However, they have escalated government anxiety around information security. As we receive more information via the Internet, it becomes harder to know what is true. Through any single major news outlet, it's almost impossible to know the origin of the information, its validity, or whether the publisher (or the publisher's owner) has their own agenda.

We're inundated with articles that have headlines like Drinking coffee causes cancer, only to find out that the headline links to another potentially unsubstantiated research study? When you see headlines like like Police 'could have done more' to stop attack, those quotation marks are only there to cordon off the parts that are hearsay - usually you'll see "alleges so-and-so person" later in the article.

As well researched and unbiased as it purports to be, all News carries an opinion. Every writer has an agenda, as do their editors, and the owners of their publications. And the information you leave out is often just as revealing as outright deception. The UK's Daily Mail is infamous for its xenophobia, and runs frequent stories on foreign workers stealing jobs, committing violent crime and abusing welfare benefits. The 2013 headline 4,000 foreign murderers and rapists we can't throw out... and, yes, you can blame human rights again is typical is typical of the Mail. You will struggle to find it covering stories on the vast economic and cultural value of immigration on the UK. Most people have very limited resources to seek out the truth of a matter for themselves. In a world where news is reported from almost every corner of the world by competing government bodies and news agencies, we can't expect anyone to travel around for themselves checking information.

This is where one of the most democratising forces to come out of the 21st century has been able to help immensely. **Citizen Journalism**, where eyewitnesses write, tweet, photograph or record what is going around them as it happens, is one of the most powerful forces in the verification of reports from established news sources. Due to the sheer number of people posting accounts or videos of what was happening in somewhere like Syria or Libya during their revolutions (or in London during the 2009 G20 protests) it becomes impossible for any one source to control the message. Consequently, it becomes far easier to hone in on what is actually happening, at least in public. It becomes impossible for a government to credibly claim it is maintaining order and peace if citizens are posting photos of military attacks and bloodshed. It becomes difficult for a government to deny accusations of torture when whistleblowers post photos anonymously via Twitter. Citizen journalism is enabled through widespread access to the internet, and happens across whichever smartphones or social networks are available. It is helping not only to democratise and corroborate established news sources, but also deconstructing the often hidden agendas that skew reporting, whether comes from state-controlled media or a national newspaper. Put simply, it is giving more power to individuals to expose injustice, and making it hard for totalitarian institutions to suppress information.

Moving Online

Growing access to knowledge provides the opportunity for anyone who can get online to learn. Through the **open-sourcing of MIT lectures, or programming courses from Stanford**, world-leading education is being made available for free to anyone who has the time and ability to view it. As courses by **Khan Academy**, or **Coursera**, or **Code Academy**, or **Udacity** gain respect and become more mainstream, they not only provide the opportunity to learn, but also the kind of credibility any qualification requires to get you a job. All degrees were not created equal, and in the same way that Harvard is more respected than the university of Hull, online courses still have a way to go before they are synonymous with quality and competence for graduating students.

What traditional universities maintain are hugely valuable networking opportunities. Anyone in the world may be able to access Stanford's curriculum, but what they can't do is meet other Stanford students, the university's famous alumni, or get introductions to potential employers. In many ways online social networks feel like they have taken over the world, but there is still not yet a substitute for meeting people and building relationships in person. Interestingly, it's often online games like **Minecraft** or **World of Warcraft**, rather than networks like Facebook, where people forge the strongest connections to strangers. Rather than just managing and 'digitising' existing relationships, online games allow people to meet new people from across the world, and put them in a situation where they have to accomplish a challenge together. Many news stories and bewildered parents lament their children spending all day and night on their computer, talking to 'strangers' and not participating in society. Online gaming and social networking, though, offer access to a far broader spectrum of people than your own neighbourhood, and the ability to connect with that community in a way that you probably don't with the people who live a few doors down. People may be interacting less with their local community, but that doesn't mean they don't feel like a valuable member of a community. These social networks are big and small at the same time. They encompass a far broader cross-section of humanity than your neighbourhood, and yet the internet allows you to select a small group that you identify with, and share your interests with them. The new wave of social networks - like **State** in the UK - have tried to incorporate this idea, connecting people with strangers through shared interests and passions.

The prevalence of online communities, and the sophistication of digital technology, economies and experiences are nowhere near the level where they provide an alternative to existence in the real world. We are far away from the world of Total Recall, where humans can have lives and experiences entirely discreet from their offline existence. However, Facebook recently acquired virtual reality company Oculus Rift, with a vision to bring a more immersive experience to their platform. And in the real world 'augmented reality' devices like Google Glass are providing a digital overlay for our physical lives.

Charter Cities

For the foreseeable future, though, our physical bodies and physical locations are here to stay. The idea of living more and more in a virtual world still causes us a great deal of anxiety and...well...we're not leaving our physical bodies any time soon. The disruptive effects of these emerging technologies on governments, though, has been vast. Multinational companies and loose international organisations (groups like Wikileaks and Anonymous) now have audiences and customers in a hundred foreign countries, and are outside of the control (and regular taxation) of almost all of them. An interesting example of the threat this represents, and how governments are reacting to it, came in 2012 with the UK government's attack on Starbucks, Google and Amazon, claiming that these multinational companies - although in full compliance with the law - were 'immoral' because they made money in UK territory, but paid proportionally less tax than local companies. Labeling these companies 'immoral' rather than using any legal basis for demanding more money shows the limitations these governments face. Governments of nation states need three things to survive – a geographical boundary, the capacity to enforce laws, and economic growth from its citizens. The decentralizing nature of these technologies is a direct threat to all three:

- Anyone with an Android smartphone, anywhere in the world, can download my app and buy things from me.
- If I live in a foreign country, it is costly and legally difficult to enforce local laws upon me.
- If citizens of another country are giving me money, or making money for me, then a foreign country is essentially 'losing revenue' by missing out on taxes.

Countries are changing, and there are many organizations exploring ways in which a small community could live within an existing state, but enjoy a degree of independence.
The idea of a **charter city** is not a new one - the idea has been suggested in developing countries for many years. Here, with the blessing or at least permission of the state, a community would establish itself with different laws and different means of decision making and law enforcement.

Post-independence America unintentionally shared strong parallels with this system. By virtue of a fledgling federal government that didn't have the means to enforce one law across the country, it was a patchwork of such communities - some prospering and others dwindling or being subsumed. The idea, though, is that if they were premeditated and engineered, such a system would allow for communities of like-minded individuals to collaborate without having risking punishment or alienation for breaking the country's broader laws. Individuals within the city could opt-out of one system and into another, and because the cities' success would depend on having smart, industrious people, they would have a vested interest in making the cities liberal and pleasant to live in. Speaking at Google's global developer conference in 2013, CEO Larry Page expressed a desire for experimental communities like charter cities that could function as testbeds for innovation outside of existing legal constraints. Given the right initial conditions, like free migration between cities, and freedom of communication, charter cities that harmed their citizens would hemorrhage people, and those that were successful would grow. Sustainable growth would benefit the surrounding state in the form of economic growth, and a more local governance would be able to cater more specifically to the needs of inhabitants, making them happier.

You might ask why - if this is such a great idea - it hasn't happened already. One answer is that many countries are reticent to devolve power. Governments want control over regulation, and the simplest way to do that is to centralise power in one place. A second, more interesting answer is that it has happened and is happening at the moment, albeit in a less deliberate way.

Hong Kong, once under British rule, is now Chinese territory. Like several areas in China, Hong Kong is designated a 'Special Economic Zone', which means that the Chinese government has designated Hong Kong free from myriad financial and other legislation that governs much of the rest of mainland China. Because Hong Kong has historically been so valuable as a center of finance and commerce, the existing legislation would have stymied its economy, and China was loath to lose all of that potential money. Although not set up as such, Hong Kong is a kind of charter city. It may not endow its inhabitants with the kinds of liberties we like to see (free expression, freedom of migration), but it demonstrates in a modern day context that nation states, even those viewed by the international community as 'repressive' are willing to loosen regulation if the upside is large economic value. This kind of model also exist in Bangladesh, India, Malaysia, Poland, Russia and many other countries. Financially troubled countries like Greece have also explored the charter city idea to counter the economic woes they are encountering at the beginning of the 21st century. On a smaller scale, if you've seen The Wire, you might recognise this as similar to the model experimented with in 'Hamsterdam' (Season 3), where the Baltimore police legalise drug-dealing within a few blocks, to localise the activity and bring down crime and violence elsewhere.

Economists like Paul Romer have also suggested charter cities as a viable solution for tackling the misuse of aid in poor countries. They could be used by aid-giving countries to funnel money into communities where it's needed, instead of handing it to governments who might siphon it off for into military spending. The cities are neither utopian pipe-dream nor dangerously destabilizing. They're a good example of how progressive solutions, which allow more freedom and decentralised power, can benefit everyone. Set up successfully, they function as a beacon to others, and are an example of how societies could grow on their merits, due to their firepower.

Going Stateless

For some, the charter city doesn't go far enough. Organisations like **The Seasteading Institute**[48] represent one of the more radical attempts at creating new societies. The institute focuses its energy on promoting research and funding for technology that would allow the construction of independent and self-sustaining floating communities, operating in international waters, and essentially outside of state regulation. These would essentially be cities built on the water, not part of any country, with a community of citizens unbound by nationality.

In one way this concept solves the problem of where to live if you wanted to 'opt out' of a country. By building new land and basing it offshore, in international waters, the seasteads circumvent the fact that almost all land is laid claim to by some country or other. The vision is one of very limited government, with that government's power held in check by the easy opt-out nature of the community (people could just leave and go back to the land). Over time, the ideas is that the seasteads would become more efficient and productive, and attract smart, capable people away from the states they live in with the promise of more freedom and lower taxes.

It's an interesting idea, and the vision has a conceptual elegance and ambition. Practically, though, there are several big hurdles. The technology does not yet exist to have a floating city endure long periods of time at sea - stability in rough weather and durability against salt erosion

---

48   http://www.seasteading.org

are both significant factors. The cost of construction and maintenance is also incredibly high, and would be prohibitive for anyone but multi-millionaires to consider an offshore lifestyle. Thirdly, the platforms have to be able to grow with the community. Unlike land, people can't simply 'spread out'. More land has to be built to accommodate more people. As well as the technical problems, though, there are also human problems that come with the isolation of being at sea. Initial communities would be heavily reliant on the mainland for natural resources, and would psychologically have left a lot behind on land. These small communities would also be at risk from pirates, and from any existing governments who weren't happy with having them on their doorstep. There are several examples of the latter: the **Republic of Rose Island**, for example, was a state founded on a man-made platform in the Adriatic sea in 1968 by engineer Giorgio Rosa. The Italian government - claiming it was a shallow attempt to avoid taxation - sent police and tax inspectors to shut it down and destroy it, even though it was in international waters. Typically, this is the way in which attempts to build so-called 'micro-nations' have been dealt with by nearby countries - brute force. These problems could be surmounted with technological advances and progressive diplomacy but will take time. The Seasteading Institute itself acknowledges that it is a torchbearer for future generations rather than a harbinger of imminent seaborne utopia.

Another option, similar to seasteading, is making a new private state; laying claim to an unoccupied island or landmass, and declaring it sovereign. The restriction with buying land, as billionaires Richard Branson and Larry

Ellison have done with Necker island and Lanai, is that the land typically remains under the jurisdiction of the country selling it. Taking unoccupied land and claiming sovereignty us what makes it an act of legal independence. This has happened, and in 1972 millionaire Michael Oliver attempted to set up a fledgeling nation state, free from "taxation, welfare, subsidies, or any form of economic interventionism". He called it the **Republic of Minerva** and built it by shipping sand to the Minerva Reefs in the Pacific Ocean. Unfortunately for Oliver, he fell victim to the same problem as others who have tried something similar. The nearby nation (Tonga in this case) asserted ownership of the waters and landmass, and essentially dismantled his state.

Outside of existing countries, it is only really the world's big companies who have the resources to 'settle' new land without being unceremoniously shut down. In 2012 Apple was estimated to have $60bn in liquid assets, holding more capital than the United States government. Its market cap was over $640bn, larger than the GDP of Switzerland, Sweden or Austria, and its quarterly profits were close to $9bn. If a company like Apple decided it wanted to set up its own organization outside of an existing state, it is not without the assets to buy the land, or the amount of revenue that currently sustains the welfare states and public services of countries with far larger populations. Why would a big company do this? It would be free from the costs that come with being based in a governed nation state - like taxation or regulation - and would be able to set up systems of legislation and welfare more suited to its employees. Many of the large tech companies already provide medical and dental insurance, free food and travel to their employees; staff at Google are only really missing somewhere to sleep at night.

It's easy to see why this hasn't happened yet. Thousands of employees would have to be willing to make the move, and uprooting from a country would provide unprecedented international legal problems, as well as questions about if and how the new company/country could be recognised. There's also the problem that big companies are more like dictatorships than democracies, and although employees may have similar values to one another, they would have little 'voting power' around how their society was run. As this kind of country grew, there would also be the problem of succession (who rules the company after the CEO?) and how to raise a new generation who were never 'employed' by the company. Being 'born into' the company would provide the same problems we have as citizens in being given a set of rules we had no chance to 'opt into'. In the long run, this society might not look that different to existing city states, like Singapore. Still, there are indications that some companies are entertaining these kinds of ideas. As well as his comments about creating spaces for experimentation, Google CEO Larry Page intimated that an initiative called **Google Y**[49] might look at building better cities and infrastructure in the near future, with a view towards creating better governance.

Off the grid

---

49   http://goo.gl/KAg903 - The Verge: Larry Page wants a Google 2.0 that will build cities and airports, report says (2014)

One last way in which people are trying to live differently is in opt-out communities within existing states. Some countries - like the US - have vast expanses of unoccupied land, and small groups that actively choose to live unconnected from their government.

There are important things that we sacrifice if we choose to opt out of society. Efficient utilities like power, water and gas require large-scale physical infrastructure which is currently only provided by governments. The fiber-optic infrastructure that provides Internet access also requires huge investment and construction. In the majority of countries these are regulated and at least part-owned by governments, and moving away from large, centralised bodies requires smaller and more resilient solutions. No-one is going to come fix your electricity or water supply if you're living off the grid. In terms of communication, solutions like **mesh-networking** - where hundreds of devices share their connection to allow wireless connectivity over a wide area - offer the possibility of Internet access without reliance upon state-constructed fiber-optic networks or cell-towers. They do, however, still require satellites or high-altitude platforms in orbit to receive a signal, so you're going to be paying someone for your phone bill. **BRCK** is a project to provide rugged WiFi Internet anywhere in the world. But again, you need a 3G contract and a credit card.

Energy and water are harder problems. Cheap, renewable energy in the form of solar, wind, hydro or geothermal power is not yet a practical solution for small communities.

Either the power generated is far too low, or the infrastructure cost prohibitively high. Companies like **SolarAid** are working in poorer countries to produce devices that reduce reliance on dirty fossil fuels, but they don't generate the scale of energy needed to power a modern home. In terms of water, entrepreneurs like Rob McGinnis are spearheading efforts like **Oasys** to make desalination cheaper and more efficient, and engineers like Michael Pritchard are demonstrating new ways to make currently unclean water sources drinkable.

At the moment existing 'opt-out' communities are not truly independent. Notable ones, like **Freetown Christiana** in Denmark, refuse to be bounded by their country's legislation, but inhabitants still retain their passports, and deal with the rest of the country for food and consumables. The fundamental problem with true peaceful secession (giving up your passport and citizenship) is the likelihood that you would be deported or arrested. For the 'off the grid' community, there is little safeguard against re-assimilation. If the community grows it will at some point attract attention, and be regulated or disbanded by the government. Even in a less repressive society such a group would only be tolerated until it had an autonomy and power which affected its surrounding area (i.e produced its own food and energy, or processed raw materials). At this point the government would come in to regulate it, or disband using physical force under the claim that it was violating law (i.e. producing illegal substances or operating without required permits). The more repressive the state, the more likely that the response would be heavy-handed and violent, to make an example to others.

Trial and Error

Each of these projects and movements has been undertaken to protecting Difference and Independence, to help people resist dogma and oppression, and to allow people to live different lives alongside or separate from systems that do not define them. Personal privacy, and control over ourselves and our personal information is core to resisting creeping 24-hour surveillance and oppression. Opening up access to information, and allowing the billions of individuals in the world to be participant in fact-checking the mass media is a powerful way to keep governments and authorities honest, and expose corruption. Online communities that span international borders allow us to find friends, support and passions outside of states that may be repressive, or communities that we just don't identify with. And larger experiments in charter cities, community building and decentralizing governance offer progressive ways to reform our countries, rather than the cycle of violence often generated by violent revolution. As we start to provide the resources that let people live independently, we encourage societies to attract people with opportunity, rather than constrain them out of fear or necessity.

There are a million other experiments, movements and initiatives that are struggling to expose injustice and protect our freedoms - these are just a few. What they have in common are that they recognise that Difference is necessary; that subverting the desires of the people you govern negates them. Empathy - understanding that just because something is different it doesn't need to be suppressed - is how we build for everyone's interests.

What is to be done

"Don't let the bastards grind you down"
- Anon.

Difference is vitality. Radical thought has been the driving force behind invention, innovation, creativity and progress throughout human history, and if we want to own and control the change in our world we have to start by believing things can be different. Nonconformism - and a tendency towards change - is an essential counterweight to our contemporary governments, which tend towards uniformity and order.

Building a society where governance is attuned to change, and is constantly adapting to provide its people with the best chance of benefiting from change, is possible. It is not where we are right now. The way in which states have accrued and consolidated power is to the detriment and exclusion of radical thought and difference. They construct community through a prescribed system of values rather than mutual understanding, and create solidarity by encouraging the collective pursuit of an homogenous thing (wealth) rather than the unique and individualised desires that wealth is supposed to help you achieve.

The state is a reaction to Difference. Art, individuality and invention - because they are different - are transgressions.

In the eyes of a system like the state that makes them a protest.

Growing up is a process of locating yourself within the world. We form our identity from our experiences, and our identity is molded at every stage by our interactions. Difference gives our identity depth. New places broaden our horizons, and learning makes us curious to learn more; it gives us the inspiration to seek out new things, and helps us define who we want to be. The less we can explore and discover, the less we will know that things can be different for us. The more borders keep us out, or keep other people away from us, the less we will really know what we share with other people. Diversity shows us our uniqueness in the world, and uniformity encourages us to believe that we are uniform.

Countries are changing, and identity is no longer drawn along such geographical lines. The information that now flows across borders through the Internet is oxygen for people who aspire to something different, and online communities and 'international cities' have become hubs where culture can transcend country. Growing income inequality is creating cultural rifts within countries that have an ultra-rich metropolis and rusting smaller towns, but these cities are nevertheless beacons of Difference and different cultures that would have been hitherto unknowable by citizens of insular nations.

In the short term existing borders are as powerfully symbolic as they have been since animals began marking their territory, but as mobility increases and networked communication penetrates the most insular societies, our personal identity is less constrained by the notion of 'citizen'. The propaganda of patriotism becomes harder to justify when 'people like you' live all over the world, and even the traditional concept of war is crumbling. US military intervention in Afghanistan was no longer against a localised enemy with a geographically delineated homeland - al-Qaeda had no Capital to storm or nation to occupy. Ideologies span continents, and cannot be routed.

Greater control over your identity and aspirations isn't about being better than everyone else, it's about recognizing that what you want can be different, but no less valuable. Not everyone lives for struggle and passion and thunder; very few people want to be the Wolf of Wall Street or the next Steve Jobs. Yours truly - as one 'data point' - aspires to nothing more some (read most) evenings than flopping down in a big red armchair with a cup of tea (read G&T) and watching Dexter. On balance, though, we get a deeper, more prolonged sense of satisfaction from the doing things rather than having things, and having more exposure to different ideas and opinions is what helps us work out what we want to do.

How to find that thing that will satisfy you, and by extension how to achieve that sense of achievement, is not something anyone can be told. One reason the world we live in has at least some happy, fulfilled people is that what everyone wants is different. We're not all competing for the same thing. Not everyone is trying to cure cancer, and not everyone wants the gold medal for the 100m sprint. Another reason is that Difference in our community and in our work brings its own fulfillment Hammering away on a production line to perfectly panel beat a million identical car parts may be mundane, but building the door frame of a home - surrounded by people who can share their specific expertise - is rewarding and fulfilling.

The layers of our lives that go into helping us work out what we want to be are like the strata, sediment and rock under our feet. They seem solid, but really they're moving all the time. Deep down at the core are our genes, the voices of our parents, our first words and the childhood values instilled within us. Layered on top of them is our schooling and our first friends. Higher up, moving around like tectonic plates, are the shifting trends of the world that expose us to Difference. Dogma and propaganda are like rock forced from the surface down into a subduction zone - it influences the education of our own children, and layers sediment on top of our own perspectives. Global news networks expose us to the vast Difference in human experience across the world.

Empathy - the understanding that what everyone wants is different - is what allows diverse societies to thrive. Rules are necessary because selfish or violent people will always victimise and exploit the innocent, but our systems should recognise that there is no one law for every situation. Breaking the speed limit to get your pregnant wife to the delivery room is different to doing 100mph to get home and watch the game. Recreationally smoking pot in your home is different to taking a hit in a kids' playground. Our systems should reflect that - their instinct should be to change with the times, and in a world where the public can be polled by hitting a button on a smartphone, they should be responsive to the people they represent. Rather than ossifying legacy laws, and adding layer upon layer of complexity as the years go by, societies should constantly be seeking to challenge their own dogma, make what is complex comprehensible, and make laws that are broad and sweeping in their powers as constrained as humanly possible. The job of a jury is to understand the nuance of each case and deliver an appropriate decision. Instead of creating knee-jerk legislation as a reaction - like banning apps or substances or books - governments should seek to understand root causes before they operate aggressively on the symptoms.

In providing for our happiness, the societies we have are far from perfect. They were built piecemeal over thousands of years by leaders who had to kill to stay alive, and who were under the constant threat of being undermined or overthrown. They emerged from hundreds of years of varying degrees of violence between people who didn't understand one another, or who were scared of one another. It's no surprise that they bear the marks of oppression, and that they are geared towards order and uniformity of thought, rather than exploration and empathy. As a species, we've done a good job of populating the world and claiming land, so we unfortunately don't have a blank slate on which we can etch today's vision of a perfect world. As well as the world we have, many of the ideas in this book emerged from the shadows cast by the worlds imagined by utopists like Thomas More and H.G. Wells, or the dystopias of Aldous Huxley and George Orwell. But this is not a utopian vision.

More and Huxley knew the paradox inherent in the world's they were creating. More's Utopia literally translates to 'no-place', and Huxley's Brave New World was sterile in its perfection; a world in which no change was possible; where being human had no purpose, and no meaning. There is no perfect world, because as the world changes, it's people change too. Just much as no-one on earth wants quite the same thing as we do, so too each of us want something slightly different to what we wanted yesterday.

There is no ideal state, and no end-state for our societies. What we do have, though, is the knowledge that to make things better we have to change them, and that it is only by exposing ourselves to different ideas and values we can work out what we want that change to be. Nonconformism - challenging the dogma we're born into - is how we start that change, and also how we protect it. Exposing ourselves to new ideas and people is how grow, and how we learn to do things differently. And empathy is what helps us change things for the better, by understanding and protecting the needs and desires of others. Every legal reform and protest speech and child born in a new country is proof that the change you want to see - and who you want to be - can be a reality. Many of these changes are likely happening somewhere in the world as you read, and the Internet means that you can probably track them down.

Happiness is not satisfaction. Satisfaction comes when you have enough to keep you secure, and if we are secure but not fulfilled then doubt - and a feeling of inadequacy -

begins to gnaw at us. Happiness comes when we are given the opportunity to discover what makes us happy, and the ability to pursue whatever that is. Realising and doing those things is what helps us to feel content. For some people that comes in running a successful business, for some designing furniture, or building rockets, or being a news reporter in a war-zone, or raising children.

It's really hard to work out what you actually want to do, and there are 1,000 voices telling you every day what you should do, and who you should be. Porsche tells you that you need a sports car; The X Factor tells you you should be famous. Everyone seems to know what will make you happy, but they are wrong.

Think about what has to change to make you and your loved ones happy, and strive to make that change. Realise the difference between what you want to do and what you are being told to do.

Realise that you don't have to do as you are told.

About the Author:

For reasons explored in depth in End States, Ben Wallace tends to avoid labels. For several years he led civic innovation and governance projects at Google, and he now advises businesses in the UK and Silicon Valley. Wallace publishes on Medium[50] and writes whenever he can. He keeps a record of projects and experiments on his website, ThisIsBangWallace[51], but little public record of the vast gratitude and love he has for his parents, who taught him what it means to be yourself.

He enjoys playing saxophone and Liar's Dice, and currently lives in San Francisco.

---

50   [50] https://medium.com/@bangwallace
51   [51] https://thisisbangwallace.appspot.com

www.ingramcontent.com/pod-product-compliance
Lightning Source LLC
Chambersburg PA
CBHW062002280526
45787CB00005B/1967